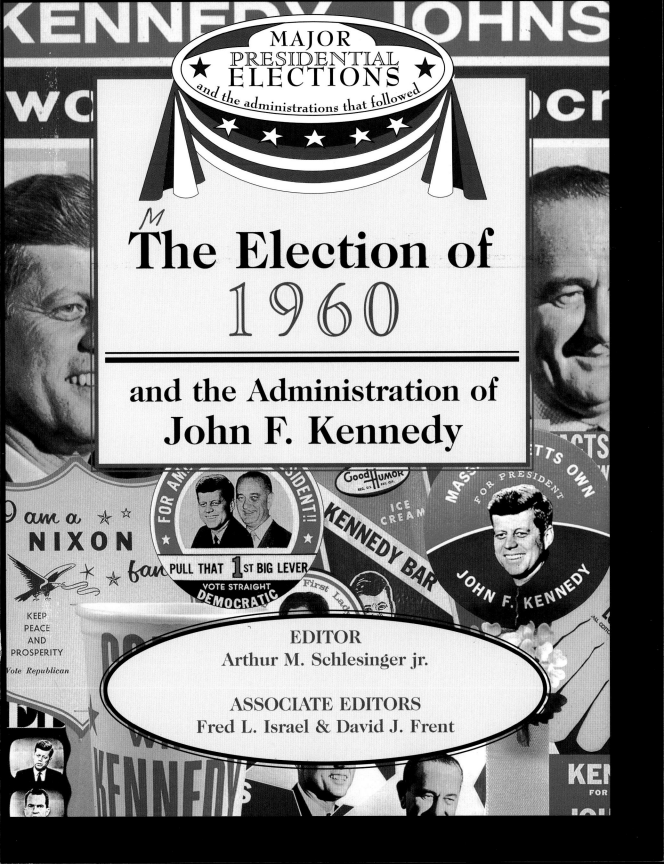

MAJOR PRESIDENTIAL ELECTIONS
and the administrations that followed

The Election of
1960

and the Administration of
John F. Kennedy

EDITOR
Arthur M. Schlesinger jr.

ASSOCIATE EDITORS
Fred L. Israel & David J. Frent

The Elections of 1789 & 1792 and the Administration of George Washington

The Election of 1800 and the Administration of Thomas Jefferson

The Election of 1828 and the Administration of Andrew Jackson

The Election of 1840 and the Harrison/Tyler Administrations

The Election of 1860 and the Administration of Abraham Lincoln

The Election of 1876 and the Administration of Rutherford B. Hayes

The Election of 1896 and the Administration of William McKinley

The Election of 1912 and the Administration of Woodrow Wilson

The Election of 1932 and the Administration of Franklin D. Roosevelt

The Election of 1948 and the Administration of Harry S. Truman

The Election of 1960 and the Administration of John F. Kennedy

The Election of 1968 and the Administration of Richard Nixon

The Election of 1976 and the Administration of Jimmy Carter

The Election of 1980 and the Administration of Ronald Reagan

The Election of 2000 and the Administration of George W. Bush

The Election of
1960

and the Administration of John F. Kennedy

EDITOR

Arthur M. Schlesinger, jr.
Albert Schweitzer Chair in the Humanities
The City University of New York

★

ASSOCIATE EDITORS

Fred L. Israel
Department of History
The City College of New York

David J. Frent
The David J. and Janice L. Frent
Political Americana Collection

Mason Crest Publishers
Philadelphia

Produced by OTTN Publishing, Stockton, New Jersey

Mason Crest Publishers
370 Reed Road
Broomall PA 19008
www.masoncrest.com

Research Consultant: Patrick R. Hilferty
Editorial Assistant: Jane Ziff

2003231

First printing

1 3 5 7 9 8 6 4 2

Library of Congress Cataloging-in-Publication Data

The election of 1960 and the administration of John F. Kennedy / editor, Arthur M. Schlesinger Jr.;
associate editors, Fred L. Israel & David J. Frent.
    p. cm. — (Major presidential elections and the administrations that followed)
Summary: A discussion of the presidential election of 1960 and the subsequent administration of
John F. Kennedy, based on source documents.
    Includes bibliographical references and index.
    ISBN 1-59084-361-4
1. Presidents—United States—Election—1960—Juvenile literature. 2. Presidents—United
States—Election—1960—Sources—Juvenile literature. 3. Kennedy, John F. (John Fitzgerald),
1917-1963—Juvenile literature. 4. United States—Politics and government—1961-1963—
Juvenile literature. 5. United States—Politics and government—1961-1963—Sources—Juvenile
literature. [1. Presidents—Election—1960—Sources. 2. Kennedy, John F. (John Fitzgerald), 1917-
1963. 3. Elections. 4. United States—Politics and government—1961-1963—Sources.]
I. Schlesinger, Arthur Meier, 1917-   II. Israel, Fred L. III. Frent, David J. IV. Series.
E837.7 .E44 2002
973.922'092—dc21
                                                                          2002012635

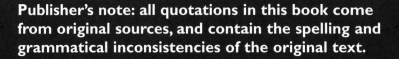

Publisher's note: all quotations in this book come
from original sources, and contain the spelling and
grammatical inconsistencies of the original text.

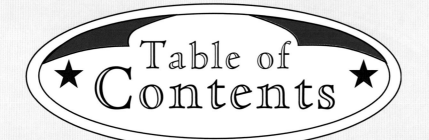

Table of Contents

★ INTRODUCTION ★
Arthur M. Schlesinger, Jr.

America suffers from a sort of intermittent fever—what one may call a quintan ague.
Every fourth year there come terrible shakings, passing into the hot fit of the presi-
dential election; then follows what physicians call "the interval"; then again the fit.

—James Bryce, *The American Commonwealth* (1888)

Running for president is the central rite in the American political order. It was not always so. *Choosing* the chief magistrate had been the point of the quadrennial election from the beginning, but it took a long while for candidates to *run* for the highest office in the land; that is, to solicit, visibly and actively, the support of the voters. These volumes show through text and illustration how those aspiring to the White House have moved on from ascetic self-restraint to shameless self-merchandising. This work thereby illuminates the changing ways the American people have conceived the role of their President. I hope it will also recall to new generations some of the more picturesque and endearing dimensions of American politics.

The primary force behind the revolution in campaign attitudes and techniques was a development unforeseen by the men who framed the Constitution—the rise of the party system. Party competition was not at all their original intent. Quite the contrary: inspired at one or two removes by Lord Bolingbroke's British tract of half a century earlier, *The Idea of a Patriot King*, the Founding Fathers envisaged a Patriot President, standing above party and faction, representing the whole people, offering the nation non-partisan leadership virtuously dedicated to the common good.

The ideal of the Patriot President was endangered, the Founding Fathers believed, by twin menaces—factionalism and factionalism's ugly offspring, the demagogue. Party competition would only encourage unscrupulous men to appeal to popular passion and prejudice. Alexander Hamilton in the 71st Federalist bemoaned the plight of the people, "beset as they continually are . . . by the snares of the ambitious, the avaricious, the desperate, by the artifices of men who possess their confidence more than they deserve it, and of those who seek to possess rather than to deserve it."

Pervading the Federalist was a theme sounded explicitly both in the first paper and the last: the fear that unleashing popular passions would bring on "the military despotism of a victorious demagogue." If the "mischiefs of faction" were, James Madison admitted in the Tenth Federalist, "sown in the nature of man," the object of politics was to repress this insidious disposition, not to yield to it. "If I could not go to heaven but with a party," said Thomas Jefferson, "I would not go there at all."

So the Father of his Country in his Farewell Address solemnly warned his countrymen against "the baneful effects of the spirit of party." That spirit, Washington conceded, was "inseparable from our nature"; but for popular government it was "truly their worst enemy." The "alternate domination of one faction over another," Washington said, would lead in the end to "formal and permanent despotism." The spirit of a party, "a fire not to be quenched . . . demands a uniform vigilance to prevent its bursting into a flame, lest, instead of warming, it should consume."

Yet even as Washington called on Americans to "discourage and restrain" the spirit of party, parties were beginning to crystallize around him. The eruption of partisanship in defiance of such august counsel argued that party competition might well serve functional necessities in the democratic republic.

After all, honest disagreement over policy and principle called for candid debate. And parties, it appeared, had vital roles to play in the consummation of the Constitution. The distribution of powers among three equal branches inclined the national government toward a chronic condition of stalemate. Parties offered the means of overcoming the constitutional separation of powers by coordinating the executive and legislative branches and furnishing the connective tissue essential to effective government. As national associations, moreover, parties were a force against provincialism and separatism. As instruments of compromise, they encouraged, within the parties as well as between them, the containment and mediation of national quarrels, at least until slavery broke the parties up. Henry D. Thoreau cared little enough for politics, but he saw the point: "Politics is, as it were, the gizzard of society, full of grit and gravel, and the two political parties are its two opposite halves, which grind on each other."

Furthermore, as the illustrations in these volumes so gloriously remind us, party competition was a great source of entertainment and fun—all the more important in those faraway days before the advent of baseball and football, of movies and radio and television. "To take a hand in the regulation of society and to discuss it," Alexis de Tocqueville observed when he visited America in the 1830s, "is his biggest concern and, so to speak, the only pleasure an American knows. . . . Even the women frequently attend public meetings and listen to political harangues as a recreation from their household labors. Debating clubs are, to a certain extent, a substitute for theatrical entertainments."

Condemned by the Founding Fathers, unknown to the Constitution, parties nonetheless imperiously forced themselves into political life. But the party system rose from the bottom up. For half a century, the first half-dozen Presidents continued to hold themselves above party. The disappearance of the Federalist Party after the War of 1812 suspended party competition. James Monroe, with no opponent at all in the election of 1820, presided proudly over the Era of Good Feelings, so called because there were no parties around to excite ill feelings. Monroe's successor, John Quincy Adams, despised electioneering and inveighed against the "fashion of peddling for popularity by traveling around the country gathering crowds together, hawking for public dinners, and spouting empty speeches." Men of the old republic believed presidential candidates should be men who already deserved the people's confidence rather than those seeking to win it. Character and virtue, not charisma and ambition, should be the grounds for choosing a President.

Adams was the last of the old school. Andrew Jackson, by beating him in the 1828 election, legitimized party politics and opened a new political era. The rationale of the new school was provided by Jackson's counselor and successor, Martin Van Buren, the classic philosopher of the role of party in the American democracy. By the time Van Buren took his own oath of office in 1837, parties were entrenched as the instruments of American self-government. In Van Buren's words, party battles "rouse the sluggish to exertion, give increased energy to the most active intellect, excite a salutary vigilance over our public functionaries, and prevent that apathy which has proved the ruin of Republics."

Apathy may indeed have proved the ruin of republics, but rousing the sluggish to exertion proved, ironically, the ruin of Van Buren. The architect of the party system became the first casualty of the razzle-dazzle campaigning the system quickly generated. The Whigs' Tippecanoe-and-Tyler-too campaign of 1840 transmuted the democratic Van Buren into a gilded aristocrat and assured his defeat at the polls. The "peddling for popularity" John Quincy Adams had deplored now became standard for party campaigners.

But the new methods were still forbidden to the presidential candidates themselves. The feeling lingered from earlier days that stumping the country in search of votes was demagoguery beneath the dignity of the presidency. Van Buren's code permitted—indeed expected—parties to inscribe their creed in plat-forms and candidates to declare their principles in letters published in news-papers. Occasionally candidates—William Henry Harrison in 1840, Winfield Scott in 1852—made a speech, but party surrogates did most of the hard work.

As late as 1858, Van Buren, advising his son John, one of the great popular orators of the time, on the best way to make it to the White House, emphasized the "rule . . . that the people will never make a man President who is so importunate as to show by his life and conversation that he not only has an eye on, but is in active pursuit of the office. . . . No man who has laid himself out for it, and was unwise enough to let the people into his secret, ever yet obtained it. Clay, Calhoun, Webster, Scott, and a host of lesser lights, should serve as a guide-post to future aspirants."

The continuing constraint on personal campaigning by candidates was reinforced by the desire of party managers to present their nominees as all things to all men. In 1835 Nicholas Biddle, the wealthy Philadelphian who had been Jackson's mortal opponent in the famous Bank War, advised the Whigs not to let General Harrison "say one single word about his principles or his creed. . . . Let him say nothing, promise nothing. Let no committee, no convention, no town meeting ever extract from him a single word about what he thinks now, or what he will do hereafter. Let the use of pen and ink be wholly forbidden as if he were a mad poet in Bedlam."

We cherish the memory of the famous debates in 1858 between Abraham Lincoln and Stephen A. Douglas. But those debates were not part of a presidential election. When the presidency was at stake two years later, Lincoln gave no campaign speeches on the issues darkly dividing the country. He even expressed doubt about party platforms—"the formal written platform system," as he called it. The candidate's character and record, Lincoln thought, should constitute his platform: "On just such platforms all our earlier and better Presidents were elected."

However, Douglas, Lincoln's leading opponent in 1860, foreshadowed the future when he broke the sound barrier and dared venture forth on thinly disguised campaign tours. Yet Douglas established no immediate precedent. Indeed, half a dozen years later Lincoln's successor, Andrew Johnson, discredited presidential stumping by his "swing around the circle" in the midterm election of 1866. "His performances in a western tour in advocacy of his own election," commented Benjamin F. Butler, who later led the fight in Congress for Johnson's impeachment, ". . . disgusted everybody." The tenth article of impeachment charged Johnson with bringing "the high office of the President of the United States into contempt, ridicule, and disgrace" by delivering "with a loud voice certain intemperate, inflammatory, and scandalous harangues . . . peculiarly indecent and unbecoming in the Chief Magistrate of the United States."

Though presidential candidates Horatio Seymour in 1868, Rutherford B. Hayes in 1876, and James A. Garfield in 1880 made occasional speeches, only Horace Greeley in 1872, James G. Blaine in 1884, and most spectacularly, William Jennings Bryan in 1896 followed Douglas's audacious example of stumping the country. Such tactics continued to provoke disapproval. Bryan, said John Hay, who had been Lincoln's private secretary and was soon to become McKinley's secretary of state, "is begging for the presidency as a tramp might beg for a pie."

Respectable opinion still preferred the "front porch" campaign, employed by Garfield, by Benjamin Harrison in 1888, and most notably by McKinley in 1896. Here candidates received and addressed numerous delegations at their own homes—a form, as the historian Gil Troy writes, of "stumping in place."

While candidates generally continued to stand on their dignity, popular campaigning in presidential elections flourished in these years, attaining new heights of participation (82 percent of eligible voters in 1876 and never once from 1860 to 1900 under 70 percent) and new wonders of pyrotechnics and ballyhoo. Parties mobilized the electorate as never before, and political iconography was never more ingenious and fantastic. "Politics, considered not as the science of government, but as the art of winning elections and securing office," wrote the keen British observer James Bryce, "has reached in the United States a development surpassing in elaborateness that of England or France as much as the methods of those countries surpass the methods of

Servia or Roumania." Bryce marveled at the "military discipline" of the parties, at "the demonstrations, the parades and receptions, the badges and brass bands and triumphal arches," at the excitement stirred by elections—and at "the disproportion that strikes a European between the merits of the presidential candidate and the blazing enthusiasm which he evokes."

Still the old taboo held back the presidential candidates themselves. Even so irrepressible a campaigner as President Theodore Roosevelt felt obliged to hold his tongue when he ran for reelection in 1904. This unwonted abstinence reminded him, he wrote in considerable frustration, of the July day in 1898 when he was "lying still under shell fire" during the Spanish-American War. "I have continually wished that I could be on the stump myself."

No such constraint inhibited TR, however, when he ran again for the presidency in 1912. Meanwhile, and for the first time, *both* candidates in 1908—Bryan again, and William Howard Taft—actively campaigned for the prize. The duties of the office, on top of the new requirements of campaigning, led Woodrow Wilson to reflect that same year, four years before he himself ran for President, "Men of ordinary physique and discretion cannot be Presidents and live, if the strain be not somehow relieved. We shall be obliged always to be picking our chief magistrates from among wise and prudent athletes,—a small class."

Theodore Roosevelt and Woodrow Wilson combined to legitimate a new conception of presidential candidates as active molders of public opinion in active pursuit of the highest office. Once in the White House, Wilson revived the custom, abandoned by Jefferson, of delivering annual state of the union addresses to Congress in person. In 1916 he became the first incumbent President to stump for his own reelection.

The activist candidate and the bully-pulpit presidency were expressions of the growing democratization of politics. New forms of communication were reconfiguring presidential campaigns. In the nineteenth century the press, far more fiercely partisan then than today, had been the main carrier of political information. In the twentieth century the spread of advertising techniques and the rise of the electronic media—radio, television, computerized public opinion polling—wrought drastic changes in the methodology of politics. In particular the electronic age diminished and now threatens to dissolve the historic role of the party.

The old system had three tiers: the politician at one end; the voter at the other; and the party in between. The party's function was to negotiate between the politician and the voters, interpreting each to the other and providing the link that held the political process together. The electric revolution has substantially abolished the sovereignty of the party. Where once the voter turned to the local party leader to find out whom to support, now he looks at television and makes up his own mind. Where once the politician turned to the local party leader to find out what people are thinking, he now takes a computerized poll.

The electronic era has created a new breed of professional consultants, "handlers," who by the 1980s had taken control of campaigns away from the politicians. The traditional pageantry—rallies, torchlight processions, volunteers, leaflets, billboards, bumper stickers—is now largely a thing of the past. Television replaces the party as the means of mobilizing the voter. And as the party is left to wither on the vine, the presidential candidate becomes more pivotal than ever. We shall see the rise of personalist movements, founded not on historic organizations but on compelling personalities, private fortunes, and popular frustrations. Without the stabilizing influence of parties, American politics would grow angrier, wilder, and more irresponsible.

Things have changed considerably from the austerities of the old republic. Where once voters preferred to call presumably reluctant candidates to the duties of the supreme magistracy and rejected pursuit of the office as evidence of dangerous ambition, now they expect candidates to come to them, explain their views and plead for their support. Where nonpartisan virtue had been the essence, now candidates must prove to voters that they have the requisite "fire in the belly." "'Twud be inth'restin," said Mr. Dooley, ". . . if th' fathers iv th' counthry cud come back an' see what has happened while they've been away. In times past whin ye voted f'r prisident ye didn't vote f'r a man. Ye voted f'r a kind iv a statue that ye'd put up in ye'er own mind on a marble pidistal. Ye nivir heerd iv George Wash'nton goin' around th' counthry distributin' five cint see-gars."

We have reversed the original notion that ambition must be disguised and the office seek the man. Now the man—and soon, one must hope, the woman— seeks the office and does so without guilt or shame or inhibition. This is not necessarily a degradation of democracy. Dropping the disguise is a gain for candor, and personal avowals of convictions and policies may elevate and educate the electorate.

On the other hand, the electronic era has dismally reduced both the intellectual content of campaigns and the attention span of audiences. In the nineteenth century political speeches lasted for a couple of hours and dealt with issues in systematic and exhaustive fashion. Voters drove wagons for miles to hear Webster and Clay, Bryan and Teddy Roosevelt, and felt cheated if the famous orator did not give them their money's worth. Then radio came along and cut political addresses down first to an hour, soon to thirty minutes—still enough time to develop substantive arguments.

But television has shrunk the political talk first to fifteen minutes, now to the sound bite and the thirty-second spot. Advertising agencies today sell candidates with all the cynical contrivance they previously devoted to selling detergents and mouthwash. The result is the debasement of American politics. "The idea that you can merchandise candidates for high office like breakfast cereal," Adlai Stevenson said in 1952, "is the ultimate indignity to the democratic process."

Still Bryce's "intermittent fever" will be upon us every fourth year. We will continue to watch wise if not always prudent athletes in their sprint for the White House, enjoy the quadrennial spectacle and agonize about the outcome.

"The strife of the election," said Lincoln after his reelection in 1864, "is but human-nature practically applied to the facts. What has occurred in this case, must ever recur in similar cases. Human-nature will not change."

Lincoln, as usual, was right. Despite the transformation in political methods there remains a basic continuity in political emotions. "For a long while before the appointed time has come," Tocqueville wrote more than a century and a half ago, "the election becomes the important and, so to speak, the all-engrossing topic of discussion. Factional ardor is redoubled, and all the artificial passions which the imagination can create in a happy and peaceful land are agitated and brought to light. . . .

"As the election draws near, the activity of intrigue and the agitation of the populace increase; the citizens are divided into hostile camps, each of which assumes the name of its favorite candidate; the whole nation glows with feverish excitement; the election is the daily theme of the press, the subject of every private conversation, the end of every thought and every action, the sole interest of the present.

"It is true," Tocqueville added, "that as soon as the choice is determined, this ardor is dispelled, calm returns, and the river, which had nearly broken its banks, sinks to its usual level; but who can refrain from astonishment that such a storm should have arisen?"

The election storm in the end blows fresh and clean. With the tragic exception of 1860, the American people have invariably accepted the result and given the victor their hopes and blessings. For all its flaws and follies, democracy abides.

Let us now turn the pages and watch the gaudy parade of American presidential politics pass by in all its careless glory.

The Election of 1960

Gil Troy is the author of *See How They Ran: The Changing Role of the Presidential Candidate* (1991) and *Mr. and Mrs. President: From the Trumans to the Clintons* (2000). He is professor of history at McGill University.

The presidential campaign of 1960 promised to revolutionize American politics. As President Dwight D. Eisenhower approached his 70th birthday and the end of his second term, a new generation of leaders emerged. Born in the twentieth century, these urban sophisticates were freer of party commitments and more comfortable on television. They embraced a modern campaigning style.

One of these leaders, Vice President Richard M. Nixon, had spent eight years paying his dues—wooing party leaders, serving as Eisenhower's hatchet-man, representing the United States abroad. Most notably, during his July 1959 visit to Moscow, Nixon had clashed with the Soviet Premier Nikita Khrushchev. In this "Kitchen Debate," the vigorous young American defended capitalism's sparkling technologies and essential freedoms before the gruff pig-breeder-turned-Communist-party-boss. Nixon trusted that such triumphs solidified his image as a statesman and would prove once and for all that he was not "Tricky Dick."

Having dispatched a last-minute convention challenge from New York's Governor Nelson Rockefeller, Nixon entered the campaign confidently. The 47-year-old Californian distanced himself from "old fashioned" partisan politics. He would emphasize not the "man" over "the party," but "issues" over "personalities."

Still, Nixon had to tread carefully. The vice president had to champion the Eisenhower administration without being too defensive. He had to inject passion into the campaign without being unstatemanlike. And he had to project confidence without stirring memories of Thomas Dewey's smug 1948 campaign. To prove, he recalled, "that a Republican campaign could be exciting and even inspiring," Nixon pledged in his acceptance speech to campaign in all fifty states.

The Democratic nominee had to work harder for his nomination.

WILL IT SPLIT?

Postcard. During the 1960 campaign, northern liberal supporters of Kennedy and some southern supporters of Lyndon B. Johnson had different interpretations of the Democratic Party's civil rights platform plank.

Estes Kefauver's early victories over Adlai Stevenson in 1956 made primaries the new springboards for popular candidacies. Harvard-educated, a World War II hero, scion of a legendary family, Senator John F. Kennedy treated the primary campaign as a dry run for the general election. Kennedy and his brother and campaign manager Robert constructed a soon-to-be-legendary machine. They built the campaign on a pile of experts. Harvard professors helped write the candidate's address; speech tutors improved his delivery; social psychologists assessed his crowds; and pollsters charted his popularity. "All I have to do is show up," Kennedy marveled, in a tribute to the "unsung heroes" of his campaign, the advance men who arranged each appearance down to the color of the bunting.

Victories in the Wisconsin and West Virginia primaries catapulted Kennedy to the nomination, as the flashy Massachusetts senator upstaged his solid but loquacious rival, Senator Hubert H. Humphrey of Minnesota. The race exhausted Kennedy and earned him wry invitations from Republicans to "drop in" on the Senate some time. But the primaries helped defuse the anti-Catholic prejudice that threatened Kennedy's efforts. Shrewdly and to Humphrey's frustration, Kennedy made the primaries a referendum, equating a vote for Kennedy with a vote for religious tolerance.

While campaigning, Kennedy learned about the country. In West Virginia, tanned and relaxed from a quick vacation in Montego Bay, Kennedy encountered Appalachian poverty. "Imagine," he said to an aide, "just imagine kids who never drink milk." Such discoveries sensitized Kennedy to the needs of the underprivileged, and proved that stumping could enlighten the candidate as well as the people.

Still, Kennedy entered the fall campaign as the underdog. Nixon played the experienced statesman to Kennedy's upstart playboy—although they had been freshman congressmen together in 1947. Kennedy looked forward to facing Nixon, who had already revealed his unique capacity to inspire hatred among Democrats. Kennedy should project a sense of "calm, dignity and command of the situation," strategists advised, "avoiding artificiality" while generating "excitement." In the wake of Harry Truman's

Postcard of Richard Nixon with Soviet Premier Nikita Khrushchev at the American National Exhibition in Moscow, July 24, 1959.

DICK NIXON — *The One Man to Deal With Khrushchev*

Richard Nixon served as Eisenhower's vice president for eight years (1953–61). Eisenhower gave him few formal responsibilities. However, Nixon popularized the office, especially through several well-publicized trips abroad on behalf of the president. Nixon also campaigned extensively for Republican candidates and, because of his attacks on Adlai Stevenson, the Democratic presidential nominee in 1952 and 1956, he developed the unenviable reputation of being the party's hatchet man. As a result, critics of President Eisenhower's policies found it easier to criticize Nixon's politics and personality rather than to attack the popular president.

whistle-stop tour, "the press and professionals" demanded that all candidates travel and speak "more than is either desirable or necessary," Professor John Kenneth Galbraith of Harvard wrote. Kennedy had to be "a hot campaigner" without burning out.

Nixon also mounted an energetic campaign. This hard-working grocer's son was determined to outhustle the millionaire playboy. The two candidates would push themselves, Theodore White noted, "until the choice of an American president seemed to rest more on pure glands and physical vitality than on qualities of statesmanship, reason, or eloquence." By the end, Nixon flew 65,000 miles, delivering more than 150 major speeches in 188 cities to over ten million people. His Democratic rival, speaking eight or ten times a day, traveled 44,000 miles, for a total of 229,000 since October 1959. Of the two vice presidential candidates, the Democrat Lyndon B. Johnson of Texas concentrated effectively on the South, while the Republican Henry Cabot Lodge Jr., campaigned in more leisurely fashion in the North and West.

Although Kennedy and Nixon disagreed on many substantive issues, both preferred to address broader themes. Nixon promised continuing peace and prosperity. Kennedy positioned himself as the "real leader for the sixties," the man who would get America moving again. "I think we can do better," the senator would declare. "I think this is a great country, but we can be a far greater country." These nostrums did not please everyone. Although the campaign would achieve mythic proportions in later years, many contemporaries mourned the callow candidates' jejune sloganeering. One bumper sticker announced: "Cheer up! You can't elect both of them."

Still, the Nixon campaign started strong, with a southern reception so frenzied that the venerable editor Ralph McGill declared it "the greatest thing in Atlanta since the premiere of *Gone With the Wind*." Three days later, Nixon bumped his knee on a car door. From August 29 through September 9, Nixon lay in the hospital, suffering from a knee infection. The inflamed knee and penicillin shots caused great pain, he later recalled, "but the mental suffering was infinitely worse."

To offset Nixon's name recognition, the Kennedy machine flooded the nation with campaign artifacts, including 24 million buttons, 19 million lapel tabs, 14 million brochures, 10 million bumper stickers, and 297 banners. The most popular pin proved to be a tie clasp commemorating Kennedy's Pacific war heroics on PT 109. The total cost of $805,303.67 contributed to the Democrats' $4 million deficit—25 percent more than the maximum each party was supposed to spend on the entire campaign.

Old-fashioned stumping and leafletting were upstaged by speculation about "The Great Debates" between the major party nominees. Although Nixon originally tried to avoid these unprecedented confrontations, he realized he had no choice. In its first decade, television had disappointed many Americans by its apparently chronic superficiality. Now, many were convinced, the four televised debates would make American politics meaningful, as it had been in the days of Lincoln and Douglas—forgetting, of course, that the famous debates took place during a senatorial election two years before the 1860 presidential contest.

The debates would "test" the people as well as the candidates, the journalist Marquis Childs claimed. Deprived of

Record album containing the four 1960 televised campaign debates between Kennedy and Nixon.

The 1960 election was a watershed for political ephemera of many varieties—the twilight of a tradition to be replaced by the emergence of television.

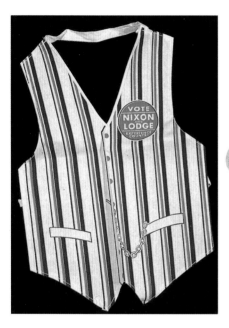

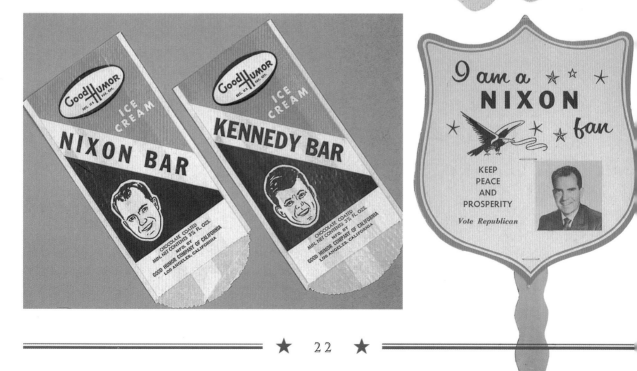

"Gunsmoke," and the "Untouchables," would "the mass audience . . . listen to a serious debates or will the ratings show a number of sets blacked out?" Before the two combatants had spoken a single word in Chicago on the night of September 26, 1960, the people had passed the test. Seventy million people stopped what they were doing, turned on their television sets and watched their leaders clash.

It quickly became apparent, however, that great expectations would not be met. The two nominees circled around each other, fearful of offending the mass audience. Years later, many would contrast the appearance of the tanned, relaxed Massachusetts senator and the ailing, five-o'clock-shadowed vice president. But at the time, more than anything else, viewers were bored. "You need a diagram to follow what they're talking about," a North Carolina housewife complained. However, by showing at least equal command of the issues, Kennedy neutralized arguments about youth and inexperience.

As the debates wound on, and benumbed commentators muttered about their redundancy, Kennedy challenged Nixon to a fifth debate. Nixon balked. His campaign had more money for a final television blitz, and he had no desire for more debates. Nixon's hesitation allowed Democrats to condemn this attempt "to keep the voters in the dark." With this move, Kennedy solidified his claim on the debates as his own, and of his victory in the debates as complete, when the debates truly were bipartisan events and were, at best, a draw.

At least 31 different studies measured public response to the debates. As the numbers proliferated, television execu-

Three Kennedy celluloid buttons. William J. Vanden Heuvel unsuccessfully ran for Congress from New York City.

tives and others rejoiced. For, as the *San Francisco Examiner* declared, "The more informed the electorate, the better for our country."

A more primitive and more integrated "living portrait" of the "whole" man emerged from the debates than from any other campaign forum, Theodore White wrote. The people now knew their candidates.

Nevertheless, the grand expectations had not been met. At best, the debates "supplement[ed]" but did not "supplant" what the *Baltimore Sun* called "the cruel grind and the inanities of conventional campaigning." "Who cares" which candidate showed "less tension" and created an "image of maturity," one voter asked. "Every good actor shows poise and appeal . . . But I have a higher regard for Abe Lincoln than I have for the actor who shot him."

In addition to the four debates, the candidates enjoyed unprecedented exposure on TV. The nightly news shows, specials, and talk shows featured the two candidates, their running mates and their families. NBC alone provided over $1.5 million worth of coverage. With the two national committees also purchasing $3 million worth of radio and television advertising time, the people

ENJOY THE PRESIDENTIAL CAMPAIGNS MORE ON A **SILVER SCREEN 85 PICTURE TUBE**

VOTE HERE FOR

• EXPERT RADIO-TV SERVICE WITH SYLVANIA TUBES
• FREE TUBE TESTING INSIDE
• PROMPT "AT-HOME" SERVICE
BE SURE TO VOTE IN NOVEMBER

An advertisement for Sylvania television sets focusing on the 1960 presidential debates.

As his 1960 running mate, Nixon chose Henry Cabot Lodge Jr., the U.S. Ambassador to the United Nations and former senator from Massachusetts. Lodge was congenial with the party's moderates and acceptable to most conservatives. However, Nixon was the man of experience. He was "Ike's boy" and better known than just about any other Republican.

learned about their nominees as never before.

Each candidate approached his advertising campaign gingerly. The Democrats were still reeling from what Frank Church of Idaho called the "barrage of bland ballyhoo" Republicans unleashed in the two Eisenhower campaigns. To demonstrate his virtue, Nixon exiled his admen to an office one block east of Madison Avenue. He refused all scripts for commercials, insisting, "I'll just sit in front of the camera and talk." Although the Democrats also claimed that their advertising agency did not "provide campaign advice or slogans," but simply "purchase[d] time and space in the commercial media," they mounted a more sophisticated effort. Commercials showcased Senator Kennedy and his wife, Jackie, in formal and informal settings and featured celebrities—including the actress Myrna Loy and the childrearing expert Dr. Benjamin Spock. One Kennedy jingle sang:

> Do you want a man for President
> Who's seasoned through and through,
> But not so doggone seasoned
>   that he won't try something new,
> And a man who's old enough to know
>   and young enough to do?
> It's up to, it's up to you
> It's strictly up to you.

All this media exposure enhanced the candidates' stumping campaigns. "The turnouts for Senator Kennedy have suddenly become impressively huge," a reporter gasped as over 600,000 people hailed the Democratic motorcade in Ohio on September 27. As Kennedy drove by, teenagers shrieked. Women sighed mindlessly, "Oh, Jack I love you, Jack, I love yuh, Jack—Jack, Jack. I love you." Broadcasting these receptions triggered

Paper campaign items from the 1960 election. The main issue of the 1960 presidential campaign became one of personality, as there appeared to be no major policy differences separating the two men. Both candidates, for example, endorsed Eisenhower's foreign policy commitments. Both promised a higher standard of living, a more workable farm program, equal rights for all citizens, and aid to education. Each claimed, however, that he could do the job better.

television's internal accelerator. Mirroring the reactions elsewhere, the crowds became even wilder. Kennedy is no longer a politician, one southern senator remarked, but a "thing," combining "the best qualities of Elvis Presley and Franklin D. Roosevelt."

Kennedy did not "have all the neurotics by any means," Taylor Grant of Mutual Broadcasting noted; Nixon was also mobbed. Ironically, both candidates had begun the campaign noted for their reserve on the stump. Nixon's famous victory wave always seemed an awkward imitation of

Celluloid button for Nixon. More than 500 varieties of buttons exist from the 1960 campaign.

Eisenhower's. Kennedy and his Ivy League advisers disdained these "folk rites." "If I have to wave both hands above my head in order to be President, I won't have the job," Kennedy confessed. It was not Kennedy or Nixon so much as television itself that transformed politicians into rock stars.

Electronic exposure altered the nature of the political audience and of the message politicians broadcast. Until now, political communication had been most effective in mobilizing partisans. All of a sudden, the campaign was reaching undecided voters. No longer simply preaching to the converted, candidates now aimed to convert the uncommitted. To achieve that, the candidates offered the fullest portrait a mass electorate had ever received. The people could "know more about" what candidates "think, their appearance, their verbal ability, their mannerisms and manners" than ever before, the *Atlanta Constitution* observed. And by moderating their message to reach more people, the candidates became more palatable. As one Minnesota farmer told the journalist Samuel Lubell after the debates, "Before I tuned in I was afraid neither man was fit to be president. But they both handled themselves well. The country will be secure with either man." According to Lubell, the stumping, the television programs, and especially the debates, "threatened to upset one of our more deeply-rooted political habits—the habit of not listening to the candidates."

As Kennedy kept his focus on the nine large states his pollster Louis Harris identified as keys to victory, Nixon found himself scrambling to reach all fifty states. From the start, Kennedy had relied on a regional strategy emphasizing the Northeast, while Nixon molded a national image. Nixon, therefore, was forced to campaign in marginal or secure states while Kennedy concentrated on strategically important ones.

On Sunday, November 6, Nixon jetted into Anchorage, Alaska, fulfilling his fifty-state pledge. Nixon heralded his great achievement as he launched a finale that Theodore White labeled the "greatest electioneering effort ever made to move men's minds." Nixon delivered fifteen-minute addresses on TV nightly. His campaign spent half-a-million dollars on a nationwide election eve telethon that had celebrities like Ginger Rogers mingling with Nixon's allies and family.

Nixon's final push featured an endorsement from Dwight Eisenhower, but it came a little too late. Eisenhower was quiet throughout the campaign. Once, when asked what major ideas the vice president had contributed to the administration, the president hesitated. "If you give me a week I might think one up," he said. As Democratic commercials replayed that snippet, many said that the president's aloofness indicated his long-standing disdain for his vice president. In his memoirs Nixon would insist that Eisenhower's doctor begged the Republican National Committee to spare the president's health and limit his campaign appearances.

Kennedy's final push received an unexpected boost when the civil rights leader Martin Luther King Jr., was arrested in

Nixon-Lodge paper sticker.

Atlanta. Both Kennedy brothers sprang into action—independently. The candidate called Mrs. King, while Robert Kennedy called the Georgia judge responsible for jailing him. The Kennedy intervention helped swing thousands of black votes to the Democrats. "I've got all my votes and I've got a suitcase, and I'm going to take him up there and dumped them in his [Kennedy's] lap," the jailed activist's father, "Daddy" King, rejoiced. A Protestant minister, King Senior confessed that "I had expected to vote against Senator Kennedy because of his religion."

The elder King was not the only American still harboring anti-Catholic prejudice. Over 300 anti-Catholic tracts, some with circulations as high as five million, blanketed the country. The Catholic Church is "Satan's superb organization on earth," they warned. Ironically, Nixon more than Kennedy tried to keep Catholicism out of the presidential campaign.

Early in the campaign, Nixon ordered "all of the people in my campaign not to discuss religion" and "not to allow anybody to participate in the campaign who does so on that ground." Although Nixon disapproved of pandering to prejudice, he also realized that the exploitation of the religious issue would be unwise. In her study of campaign advertising, Kathleen Hall Jamieson argues that Kennedy and not Nixon benefited from the issue. Democrats broadcast Kennedy's pleas for religious toleration disproportionately in

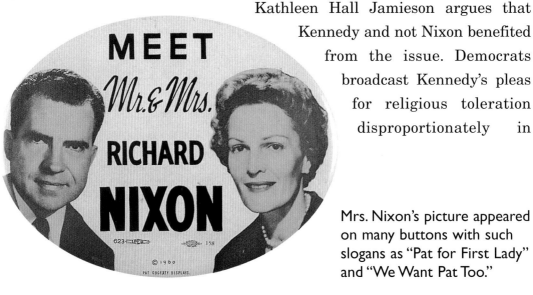

Mrs. Nixon's picture appeared on many buttons with such slogans as "Pat for First Lady" and "We Want Pat Too."

Celluloid button for the Republican candidates.

Catholic areas, less to mollify Protestants than to mobilize Catholics. The strategy worked. Some estimate that while 50 percent of Catholics voted for Adlai Stevenson in 1956, over 80 percent voted for Kennedy in 1960.

The election was one of the closest in the twentieth century. The result hung in the balance until Illinois went to Kennedy—thanks, many said, to hundreds of corpses who voted in Mayor Richard Daley's Chicago wards. (Had Kennedy lost Illinois, however, he would still have won in the electoral college.) Nixon bitterly concluded that images and tactics swayed the campaign. In his memoirs, Nixon claimed that Kennedy's campaign had "unlimited money" and was "led by the most ruthless group of political operators ever mobilized for a presidential campaign." Nixon "vowed that I would never again enter an election at a disadvantage by being vulnerable to them—or anyone—on the level of political tactics."

Americans feared that TV threatened their country's political soul. Richard Nixon's many faces proved that politicians did not know how to resolve the struggle. On the campaign trail, Nixon was at once scoundrel and saint, the prophet of calculation and virtuously oblivious. In his Checkers speech of 1952, and in a well-publicized 1955 speech, Nixon acknowledged that candidates could only achieve the intimacy and spontaneity TV demanded through careful preparation. "[T]here isn't any such thing as a non-political speech by a politician," he told broadcasting executives. But by 1960, Nixon himself was the "non-political" politician, eschewing personalities and victimized by the mysterious new medium. Only in retrospect did he "learn" to pay attention to appearances over

The 1960 presidential election saw an aged general succeeded by the youngest man ever elected president. To some, Kennedy's thousand-day presidency seems a romantic chapter in the often sordid history of American politics. He, his family, and advisers conveyed an exciting sense of elitism, a sense that the best people had been summoned forth from the country.

> The 1960 presidential election was a watershed in American political history. At 43, John Kennedy, the youngest man ever elected to the presidency and the first Catholic to hold the office, took over the power vested for eight years in Dwight Eisenhower, who, at 70, was, to that time, the oldest White House occupant. This was the first time that a major party had nominated two incumbent senators for president and vice president—Kennedy and Lyndon Johnson—and the first time that the Democrats had sent a sitting senator to the White House. In addition, Kennedy was the first Democratic presidential nominee from New England since Franklin Pierce in 1852.

issues. As techniques would become more sophisticated, and more ubiquitous, the confusion, and the doubts, would intensify.

But while many blamed the modern technology, these problems were not new. Television and advertising accelerated and nationalized the campaign—but the dissatisfaction and dilemmas stemmed from the paradoxical political system the Founding Fathers created. Americans were still not sure if they wanted style or substance in a candidate, a dignified king or a candid prime minister. The disappointments of the 1960 campaign—as with its predecessors and successors—were part of the nation's historic failure to make peace with American democracy.

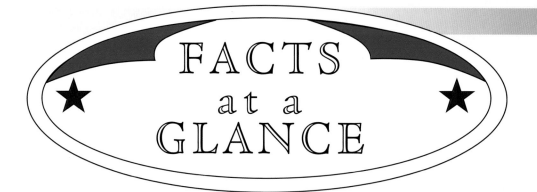

JOHN FITZGERALD KENNEDY

- **Born:** May 29, 1917, in Brookline, Massachusetts
- **Parents:** Joseph Patrick and Rose Fitzgerald Kennedy
- **Education:** Graduated from Harvard University in 1940
- **Occupation:** public official
- **Married:** Jacqueline Lee Bouvier (1929–1994) on September 12, 1953
- **Children:** Caroline Bouvier Kennedy (1957–   ); John Fitzgerald
  Kennedy, Jr. (1960–1999); Patrick Bouvier Kennedy (1963)
- **Died:** November 22, 1963, in Dallas, Texas

Served as the 35TH PRESIDENT OF THE UNITED STATES,

- January 20, 1961, to November 22, 1963

VICE PRESIDENT

- Lyndon B. Johnson (1961–63)

CABINET

Secretary of State
• Dean Rusk (1961–63)

Secretary of the Treasury
• C. Douglas Dillon (1961–63)

Secretary of Defense
• Robert S. McNamara (1961–63)

Attorney General
• Robert F. Kennedy (1961–63)

Postmaster General
• J. Edward Day (1961–63)
• John A. Gronouski, Jr. (1963)

Secretary of the Interior
• Stewart L. Udall (1961–63)

Secretary of Agriculture
• Orville L. Freeman (1961–63)

Secretary of Commerce
• Luther H. Hodges (1961–63)

Secretary of Labor
• Arthur J. Goldberg (1961–62)
• W. Willard Wirtz (1962–63)

Secretary of Health, Education, and Welfare
• Abraham A. Ribicoff (1961–62)
• Anthony J. Celebrezze (1962–63)

OTHER POLITICAL POSITIONS

• Member of U.S. House of Representatives, 1947–53
• United States Senator, 1953–61

NOTABLE EVENTS DURING KENNEDY'S ADMINISTRATION

1961   John F. Kennedy is inaugurated as the 35th president of the United States on January 20; on March 1, the president initiates the Peace Corps, which is intended to bring American skills and idealism to new and developing countries; on April 20, assumes responsibility for the failed Bay of Pigs invasion of Cuba; on May 25, speaks to Congress on "urgent needs," including an increased American space effort that will put a man on the moon by the end of the decade.

1962   In September, announces that the federal government will carry out a court order admitting James Meredith to the University of Mississippi; successfully handles the Cuban Missile Crisis, forcing the Soviet Union to back down.

1963   In June, proposes civil rights legislation that will give all Americans equal opportunity in education, employment, public accommodations, voting, and access to Federal programs; on October 7, signs the Nuclear Test Ban Treaty; on November 2, in South Vietnam Ngo Dinh Diem and his brother are killed during a military coup supported by the CIA; John F. Kennedy is assassinated on November 22 in Dallas, Texas.

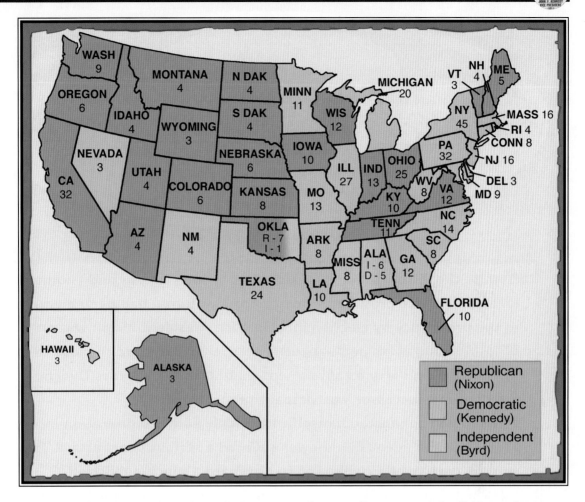

In one of the closest presidential elections in history, Democrat John F. Kennedy was elected with 303 electoral votes from 23 states to 219 electoral votes (from 26 states) for Republican Richard M. Nixon. Nationally, Kennedy won a narrow margin of about 112,000 votes; a swing of just 32,500 ballots (4,500 in Illinois and 28,000 in Texas) would have given the election to Nixon.

The division over civil rights that would erupt in violence later in the 1960s were apparent in the 1960 election. Mississippi chose eight unpledged electors, who gave their support to states' rights candidate Harry Byrd. In Oklahoma, one Republican elector voted for Byrd. In Alabama, five of the 11 presidential electors were pledged to the Democratic Party; the other six were unpledged and voted for Byrd.

Nixon Accepts the Nomination

Despite the distinguished precedent set by John Adams and Thomas Jefferson, no vice president since Martin Van Buren had been elevated to the presidency by election in 1836. Vice President Nixon was only 47 in 1960 and at his peak—experienced, articulate, and so close to the Republican Party establishment that his nomination as Dwight Eisenhower's successor was virtually preordained.

Nixon had conducted himself with widely admired discretion in late 1955 when President Eisenhower suffered a serious heart attack. This episode persuaded Eisenhower to disregard a much-publicized attempt to prevent Nixon's renomination as vice president in 1956. Also, Nixon had solidified himself with Republican leaders as he crisscrossed the nation supporting local candidates and raising money for them. From 1956 on, Nixon was the heir apparent.

In Nixon's acceptance speech at the 1960 Republican convention, he pledged to personally campaign in each of the fifty states. He outlined his vision for America—an America committed "to the cause of freedom and all it stands for." "I believe in the American dream," Nixon told an enthusiastic convention, "because I have seen it come true in my own life. . . . When Mr. Khrushchev says our grandchildren will live under Communism, let us say his grandchildren will live in freedom."

Mr. Chairman, delegates to this convention, my fellow Americans, I have made many speeches in my life, and never have I found it more difficult to find the words adequate to express what I feel, as I find them tonight.

To stand here before this great convention, to hear your expression of affection for me, for Pat, for our daughters, for my mother, for all of us who are representing our party, is, of course, the greatest moment of my life.

And I just want you to know that my only prayer as I stand here is that in the months ahead I may be in some way worthy of the affection and the trust which you have presented to me on this occasion, in everything that I say, in everything that I do, in everything that I think in this campaign and afterwards.

May I also say that I have been wanting to come to this convention, but because of the protocol that makes it necessary for a candidate not to attend the convention until the nominations are over, I have had to watch it on television. And I want all of you to know that I have never been so proud of my party as I have been in these last three days as I compared this convention, the conduct of our delegates and our speakers, with what went on in my native State of California, just two weeks ago. I congratulate Chairman Halleck and Chairman Morton and all of those who have helped to make this convention one that will stand in the annals of our party forever as one of the finest we have ever held.

Have you ever stopped to think of the memories you will take away from this convention? The things that run through my mind are these: That first day, with the magnificent speeches—Mr. Hoover with his great lessons for the American people; Walter Judd, with one of the most outstanding keynote addresses in either party in history and last night our beloved, fighting President, making the greatest speech I ever heard him make, before this convention.

Your platform and its magnificent presentation by Chuck Percy, the chairman. For these and for so many other things I want to congratulate you tonight and to thank you from the bottom of my heart and on behalf of Americans—not just Republicans, but Americans—everywhere for making us proud of our country and of our two-party system for what you have done.

Tonight, too, I particularly want to thank this convention for nominating as my running mate a world statesman of the first rank, my friend and colleague, Henry Cabot Lodge of Massachusetts. In refreshing contrast to what happened in Los Angeles you nominated a man who shares my views on the great issues and who will work with me and not against me in carrying out our magnificent platform.

And, may I say that during this week we Republicans with strong convictions about our party and about our country had our differences—but as the speech by Senator Goldwater indicated yesterday, and the elegant and gracious remarks of my friend, Nelson Rockefeller, indicated tonight, we know that the differences that divided us were infinitesimal compared to the gulf between us and what the Democrats would put upon us as a result of what they did at Los Angeles during their convention two weeks ago.

It was only eight years ago that I stood in this very place after you had nominated as our candidate for the President one of the great men of our century; and I say to you tonight that for generations to come Americans, regardless of party, will gratefully remember Dwight Eisenhower as the man who brought peace to America, as the man under whose leadership Americans enjoyed the greatest progress and prosperity in history. Above all, they will remember him as the man who restored honesty, integrity and dignity to the conduct of Government in the highest office of this land.

And, my fellow Americans, I know now that you will understand what I am about to say, because the next President of the United States will have Dwight Eisenhower's great example to follow in confronting new and challenging world problems of utmost gravity. This truly is the time for greatness in

A Gallup Poll taken immediately after both conventions had met gave Nixon a 50–44 lead with only six percent undecided. In truth, there were probably many more undecided who saw many similarities between the two candidates. Both were comparatively young and earnest men first elected to Congress in 1946—both had widely traveled abroad and preferred foreign policy over domestic problems—both were proud to be professional politicians and both were more expert in their knowledge of that profession than any of their advisors—both had an understanding of the unique importance of the presidency and a genuine dedication to advancing the national interest—both had an uneasy time attempting to please disparate factions within their respective parties—and both had, on at least one notable occasion, endured the wrath of the nation's intellectual liberals, Nixon for his zealous role on the House Un-American Activities Committee in the late 1940s and Kennedy for going unrecorded, even by "pairing," when illness caused him to miss the 1954 Senate roll-call vote censuring Senator Joseph McCarthy. Perhaps, in retrospect, Kennedy's speeches looked to the future—to the conquest of space and disease and the realization of the American dream for all while Nixon seemed to stress the preceding eight years in which the American people had, on the whole, been more prosperous and contented than ever before.

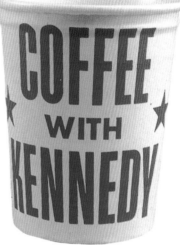

America's leadership.

I am sure you will understand why I do not say tonight that I alone am the man who can furnish that leadership. That question is not for me to decide, but for you—and I only ask that the thousands in this hall and the millions listening to me on television make that decision in the most thoughtful way you possibly can, because what you decide this November will not only affect your lives and your future, it will affect the future of millions throughout the world. I urge you to study the records of the candidates, to listen to my speeches and my opponent's and Mr. Lodge's and his opponent's, and then, after you have studied our records and listened to our speeches, decide. Decide on the basis of what we say and what we believe who is best qualified to lead America and the free world in this critical period.

To help you make this decision I would like to discuss tonight some of the great problems which will confront the next President of the United States and the policies that I believe should be adopted to meet them.

One hundred years ago, in this very city, Abraham Lincoln was nominated for President of the United States. The problems which will confront our next President will be even greater than those that confronted Lincoln. The question then was freedom for the slaves and survival of the Nation. The question now is freedom for all mankind and the survival of civilizations, and the choice that each of you listening to me makes this November can affect the answer to that question.

What should your choice be? Well, let us first examine what our opponents offered in Los Angeles two weeks ago. They claimed theirs was a new program, but you know what it was. It was simply the same old proposition that a political party should be all things to all men, and nothing more than that, and they promised everything to everybody with one exception: they didn't promise to pay the bill.

And I say tonight that with their convention, their platform, and their ticket, they composed a symphony of political cynicism which is out of harmony with our times today.

Now, we come to the key question. What should our answer be? And some might say to do as they do—out-promise them because that is the only way to win. And I want to tell you my answer. I happen to believe that their program would be disastrous for America, that it would wreck our economy, and that it would dash our people's high hopes for a better life. And I serve notice here and now that whatever the political consequences, we are not going to try to out-promise our opponents in this campaign.

We are not going to make promises we cannot and should not keep, and we are not going to try to buy the people's votes with their own money. And to those who say that this position will mean political defeat, my answer is this: We have more faith than that in the good sense of the American people, provided the people know the facts, and here is where we come in.

I pledge to you tonight that we will bring the facts home to the American people, and we will do it with a campaign such as this country has never seen before.

I have been asked all week long by the newsmen sitting on my right and left, "When is this campaign going to begin, Mr. Vice President? On Labor Day or one of the other traditional starting dates?" And this is my answer: This campaign begins tonight, here and now, and this campaign will continue from now until November 8 without any letup.

I have also been asked by my friends in the press, "Mr. Vice President, where are you going to concentrate? What States are you going to visit?" And this is my answer: In this campaign we are going to take no States for granted, and we are not going to concede any States to the opposition.

I announce to you tonight, and I pledge to you, that I personally will carry this campaign into every one of the 50 States of this Nation between now and November 8. And in this campaign I make a prediction—I say that just as in 1952 and 1956 millions of Democrats will join us, not because they are deserting their party, but because their party deserted them at Los Angeles two weeks ago.

Now, I have suggested to you what our friends of the opposition offered to the American people. What do we offer? First, we are proud to offer the best eight-year record of any administration in the history of this country. But, my fellow Americans, that isn't all and that isn't enough, because we happen to believe that a record is not something to stand on, but something to build on; and in building on the record of this administration we shall build a better America, we shall build an America in which we shall see the realization of the dreams of millions of people not only in America but throughout the world for a fuller, freer, richer life than men have ever known in the history of mankind.

Let me tell you something of the goals of this better America toward which we will strive. In this America, our older citizens shall not only have adequate protection against the hazards of ill health, but a greater opportunity to lead a useful and productive life by participating to the extent they are able in the Nation's exciting work rather than sitting on the sidelines. And in the better America, young Americans shall not only have the best basic education in America, but every boy and girl of ability, regardless of his financial circumstances, shall have the opportunity to develop his intellectual capabilities to the full. Our wage earners shall enjoy increasingly higher wages in honest dollars, with better protection against the hazards of unemployment and old age. And, for those millions of Americans who are still denied equality of rights and opportunity, I say there shall be the greatest progress in human rights since the days of Lincoln 100 years ago.

And America's farmers, to whose hard work and almost incredible efficiency we owe the fact that we are the best fed, best clothed people in the world, I say America's farmers must and will receive what they do not have today, and what they deserve—a fair share of America's ever-increasing prosperity. To accomplish these things we will develop to the full the untapped natural resources, our water, our minerals, our power with which we are so fortunate to be blessed in this rich land of ours. And we shall provide for our scientists the support they need for the research that will open exciting new highways into a future in which we shall have progress which we cannot even dream of today. Above all, in this decade of decision and progress we will witness the continued revitalization of America's moral and spiritual strength, with a renewed faith in the eternal ideals of freedom and justice under God which are our priceless heritage as a people.

Now, I am sure that many of you in this hall, and many of you watching on television, might well ask, "But Mr. Nixon, don't our opponents favor just such goals as this?" And my answer is, Yes, of course. All Americans regardless of party want a better life for our people. What is the difference then? I will tell you what it is. The difference is in the way we propose to reach these goals, and the record shows that our way works and theirs doesn't and we are going to prove it in this campaign.

We produce on the promises that they make. We succeed where they fail.

Do you know why? Because, as Governor Rockefeller said in his remarks, we put our primary reliance not upon government but upon people for progress in America. That is why we will succeed.

We must never forget that the strength of America is not in its Government, but in its people. And we say tonight there is no limit to the goals America can reach, provided we stay true to the great American traditions.

A government has a role, and a very important one, but the role of government is not to take responsibility from people, but to put responsibility on them. It is not to dictate to people, but to encourage and stimulate the creative productivity of 180 million free Americans. That is the way to progress in America.

In other words, we have faith in the people, and because our programs for progress are based on that faith, we shall succeed where our opponents will fail, in building the better America that I have described.

But if these goals are to be reached, the next President of the United States must have the wisdom to choose between the things government should and shouldn't do. He must have the courage to stand against the pressures of the few for the good of the many. And he must have the vision to press forward on all fronts for the better life our people want.

Now, I have spoken to you of the responsibilities of our next President at home. Those which he will face abroad will be infinitely greater. But before I look to the future, let me say a word about the past.

At Los Angeles two weeks ago, we heard the United States, our Government, blamed for Mr. Khrushchev's sabotage of the Paris Conference. We heard the United States blamed for the actions of Communist-led mobs in Caracas and Tokyo. We heard that American education and American scientists are inferior. We heard that America militarily and economically is a second-rate country. We heard that American prestige is at an all-time low.

This is my answer: I say that at a time the Communists are running us down abroad, it is time to speak up for America at home.

And my friends, let us recognize that America has its weaknesses, and constructive criticism of those weaknesses is essential—essential so that we can correct our weaknesses in the best traditions of our democratic process.

But let us also recognize this: While it is dangerous to see nothing wrong in America, it is just as wrong to refuse to recognize what is right about America.

And tonight I say to you no criticism should be allowed to obscure the truth either at home or abroad that today America is the strongest nation militarily, economically, ideologically in the world; and we have the will and the stamina and the resources to maintain that strength in the years ahead.

Now, turning to the future. We must recognize that the foreign policy problems of the 1960s will be different and they will be vastly more difficult than those of the 1950s through which we have just passed.

We are in a race tonight, my fellow Americans, a race for survival in which our lives, our fortunes, our liberties are at stake. We are ahead now, but the only way to stay ahead in a race is to move ahead; and the next President will make decisions which will determine whether we win or whether we lose this race.

What must he do? These things I believe: he must resolve first and above all that the United States must never settle for second best in anything.

Let us look at the specifics. Militarily, the security of the United States must be put before all other considerations. Why? Not only because this is necessary to deter aggression, but because we must make sure that we are never in a position at the conference table where Mr. Khrushchev or his successor is able to coerce an American President because of his strength and our weakness.

Diplomatically, let us look at what the problem is. Diplomatically, our next President must be firm—firm on principles; but he must never be belligerent, he must never engage in a war of words which might heat up the international climate to the igniting point of nuclear catastrophe.

But while he must never answer insults in kind, he must leave no doubt at any time that in Berlin or in Cuba or anywhere else in the world, America will not tolerate being pushed around by anybody, because we have already paid a terrible price in lives and resources to learn that appeasement leads not to peace but to war. It will indeed take great leadership to steer us through these years, avoiding the extremes of belligerency on the one hand, and appeasement on the other.

Now, Mr. Kennedy has suggested that what the world needs is young leadership; and, understandably this has great appeal, because it is true that youth does bring boldness and imagination and drive to leadership, and we need all those things. But I think most people will agree with me tonight when I say that President De Gaulle, Prime Minister Macmillan, and Chancellor Adenauer may not be young men—but we are indeed fortunate in that we have their wisdom and their experience and their courage on our side in the struggle for freedom today in the world.

And I might suggest that as we consider the relative merits of youth and age it is only fair to point out that it was not Mr. De Gaulle or Mr. Macmillan or Mr. Adenauer, but Mr. Kennedy who made the rash and impulsive suggestion that President Eisenhower could have apologized or sent regrets to Mr. Khrushchev for the U-2 flights which the President had ordered to save our country from surprise attack.

But formidable as will be the diplomatic and military problems confronting the next President, far more difficult and critical will be the decisions he must make to meet and defeat the enemies of freedom in an entirely different kind of struggle. And here I want to speak to you of another kind of aggression, aggression without war, where the aggressor comes not as a conqueror, but as a champion of peace, of freedom, offering progress and plenty and hope to the unfortunates of the earth.

I say tonight that the major problem confronting the next President of the United States will be to inform the people of the character of this kind of aggression, to arouse the people to the mortal danger it presents, and to inspire the people to meet that danger. And he must develop a brand-new strategy which will win the battle for freedom for all men and win it without a war. That is the great task of the next President of the United States. And this will be a difficult task, difficult because at times our next President must tell the people, not what they want to hear, but what they need to hear. Why, for example, it may be just as essential to the national interest to build a dam in India as in California.

It will be difficult, too, because, you know, we Americans have always been able to see and understand the danger presented by missiles and airplanes and bombs; but we have found it hard to recognize the even more deadly danger of the propaganda that warps the mind, the economic offensive that softens a nation, the subversion that destroys the will of a people to resist tyranny.

And yet, I say tonight that while this threat is, as I believe it to be, the greatest danger we have ever confronted, this is no reason for lack of confidence in the outcome.

Do you know why? Because there is one great theme that runs through our history as a Nation: "Americans are always at their best when the challenge is greatest."

And I say tonight that we Americans shall rise to our greatest heights in this decade of the sixties as we mount the offensive to meet those forces which threaten the peace and the rights of free men everywhere.

But there are some things we can do and some things we must do, and I would like to list them for you tonight:

First, we must take the necessary steps which will assure that the

American economy grows at a maximum rate so that we can maintain our present massive lead over the Communist bloc. How do we do this? There isn't any magic formula by which government in a free nation can bring this about. The way to assure maximum growth in America is not by expanding the functions of government, but by increasing the opportunities for investment and creative enterprise for millions of individual Americans.

And at a time when the Communists have found it necessary to turn to decentralization of their economy and to turn to the use of individual incentives to increase productivity—at a time, in other words, when they are turning our way—I say we must and we will not make the mistake of turning their way.

There is another step that we must take: our Government activities must be reorganized, reorganized to take the initiative from the Communists and to develop and carry out a worldwide strategy and offensive for peace and freedom.

The complex of agencies which have grown up through the years for exchange of persons, for technical assistance, for information, for loans and grants—all these must be welded together into one powerful economic and ideological striking force under the direct supervision and leadership of the United States.

Because what we must do, you see, is to wage the battles for peace and freedom with the same unified direction and dedication with which we wage battles in war. And if these activities are to succeed, we must develop a better training program for the men and women who will represent our country at home and abroad. What we need are men with a broad knowledge of the intricacies and techniques of the strategies of the Communists, with the keen knowledge of the great principles for which free people stand, and, above all, men who with a zeal and dedication which the Communists cannot match will outthink, outwork and outlast the enemies of freedom wherever they meet them anywhere in the world. This is the kind of men we must train.

And we must recognize that government cannot do this job alone. The most effective proponents of freedom are not governments, but free people; and this means that every American—every one of you listening tonight—who works or travels abroad, must represent his country at its best in everything that he does.

The United States, big as it is, strong as it is, cannot do this job alone. The best brains, the fullest resources of free nations, which have as great a stake in freedom as we have, must be mobilized to participate with us in this task to the extent they are able.

But do you know what is most important of all? Above all, we must recognize that the greatest economic strength that we can imagine, and the finest government organization—all this will fail if we are not united and inspired by a great idea, an idea which will be a battle cry for a grand offensive to win the minds and the hearts and the souls of men. Do we have such an idea?

The Communists proclaim over and over again that their aim is the victory of communism throughout the world. It is not enough for us to reply that our aim is to contain communism, to defend the free world against communism, to hold the line against communism; the only answer to a strategy of victory for the Communist world is a strategy of victory for the free world.

But let the victory we seek be not victory over any other nation or any other people. Let it be the victory of freedom over tyranny, of plenty over hunger, of health over disease, in every country of the world.

When Mr. Khrushchev says our grandchildren will live under communism, let us say his grandchildren will live in freedom. When Mr. Khrushchev says the Monroe Doctrine is dead in the Americas, we say the doctrine of freedom applies everywhere in the world.

And I say tonight let us welcome Mr. Khrushchev's challenge to peaceful competition of our systems; but let us reply, "Let us compete in the Communist world as well as in the free world," because Communist dictators must not be allowed the privileged sanctuary from which to launch their guerrilla attacks on the citadels of freedom.

And, we say further, extend this competition, extend it to include not only food and factories as he has suggested but extend it to include the great spiritual and moral values which characterize our civilization.

Also, my friends, let us welcome the challenge, not be disconcerted by it nor fail to meet it, but welcome the challenge presented by the revolution of peaceful peoples' aspirations in South America, in Africa.

We cannot fail in this mission. We cannot fail to assist them in finding a way to progress with freedom so that they will not be faced with the terrible alternative of turning to communism with its promise of progress at the cost of freedom.

Let us make it clear to them that our aim in helping them is not merely to stop communism, but that in the great American tradition of concern for those less fortunate than we are that we welcome the opportunity to work with people everywhere in helping them to achieve their aspirations for a life of human dignity. And this means that our primary aim must be not to help governments but to help people, to help people attain the life they deserve.

In essence, what I am saying tonight is that our answer to the threat of the Communist revolution is renewed devotion to the great ideals of the American Revolution, ideals that caught the imagination of the world 180 years ago and that still live in the minds and hearts of people everywhere.

I could tell you tonight that all you need to do to bring about these things that I gave just described is to elect the right man as President of this country and leave these tasks to him. But, my fellow Americans, America demands more than that of me and of you.

When I visited the Soviet Union, in every factory there was a huge sign which read, "Work for the victory of communism," and what America needs today is not just a President, not just a few leaders, but millions of Americans working for the victory of freedom. Each American must make a personal and total commitment to the cause of freedom and all it stands for. It means wage earners and employers making an extra effort to increase the productivity of our factories. It means our students in schools striving for increasing excellence rather than adjusting to mediocrity.

It means supporting and encouraging our scientists to explore the unknown, not just for what we can get but for what we can learn, and it means each American assuming a personal responsibility to make this country which we love a proud example of freedom for all the world: each of us for example, doing our part in ending the prejudice which 100 years after Lincoln, to our shame, still embarrasses us abroad and saps our strength at home; each of us participating in this and other political campaigns not just by going to the polls and voting but working for the candidate of your choice. And, my fellow Americans, it means sacrifice—not the grim sacrifice of desperation but the rewarding sacrifice of choice which lifts us out the humdrum life in which we live and gives us the supreme satisfaction which comes from working together in a cause greater than ourselves, greater than our Nation, as great as the whole world itself.

What I propose tonight is not new, it is as old as America, and as young as America, because America will never grow old. You will remember that Thomas Jefferson said, "We act not for ourselves alone, but for the whole human race." Lincoln said, "In giving freedom to these slaves we assure freedom to the free. We shall nobly save or meanly lose the last hope of the earth." And Teddy Roosevelt said, "Our first duty as citizens of the Nation is owed to the United States, but if we are true to our principles we must also think of serving the interests of mankind at large." And Woodrow Wilson said, "A patriotic American is never so proud of the flag under which he lives as when it comes to mean to others, as well as himself, a symbol of hope and liberty."

We say today that a young America shall fulfill her destiny by helping to build a new world in which men can live together in peace and justice and freedom with each other. But there is a difference today, an exciting difference, and the difference is because of the dramatic breakthrough in science for the first time in human history. We have the resources, the resources to wage a winning war against poverty, misery, and disease wherever it exists in the world.

And upon the next President of the United States will rest the responsibility to inspire and to lead the forces of freedom toward this goal.

I am sure now that you understand why I said at the beginning that it would be difficult for any man to say that he was qualified to provide this kind of leadership. I can only say to you tonight that I believe in the American dream because I have seen it come true in my own life. I know something of the threat which confronts us and I know something of the effort which will be needed to meet it. I have seen hate for America, not only in the Kremlin, but in the eyes of Communists in our own country, and on the ugly face of a mob in Caracas.

I have heard doubts about America expressed, not just by Communists, but by sincere students and labor leaders in other countries searching for the way to a better life and wondering if we had lost the way. And I have also seen love for America in countries throughout the world, in a crowd in Chicago, in Bogota, in the heart of Siberia, and in Warsaw—250,000 people on the streets on a Sunday afternoon singing, crying with tears running down their cheeks and shouting "Niech Zyje America"—Long live the United States.

And my fellow Americans, I know that we must resist the hate, we must remove the doubts, but above all we must be worthy of the love and the trust of millions on this earth for whom America is the hope of the world.

A hundred years ago, Abraham Lincoln was asked during the dark days of the tragic War Between the States whether he thought God was on his side. His answer was, "My concern is not whether God is on our side, but whether we are on God's side." My fellow Americans, may that ever be our prayer for our country. And in that spirit, with faith in America, with faith in her ideals and her people, I accept your nomination for President of the United States.

Kennedy Accepts the Nomination

John Kennedy had a difficult political fight before he won the Democratic presidential nomination. Favorites of the liberal Roosevelt / Truman wing of the party included Senator Hubert Humphrey of Minnesota and Adlai Stevenson, the former governor of Illinois who had lost twice to Eisenhower. Many Democratic moderates supported either Senator Stuart Symington of Missouri or Lyndon Johnson, the Senate majority leader.

In 1960, candidates were still chosen by party nominating conventions. Only thirteen states held presidential primaries. Still Kennedy, to overcome doubts about the winning potential of a Catholic, took on Humphrey in key primaries held in Wisconsin and West Virginia. He won both, and his 61 percent in heavily fundamentalist Protestant West Virginia gave him a commanding advantage for the Democratic nomination. Kennedy's choice of Lyndon Johnson, his most formidable rival, as his vice presidential running mate, was a master stroke— and Johnson's acceptance seemed almost as astonishing.

Governor Stevenson, Senator Johnson, Mr. Butler, Senator Symington, Senator Humphrey, Speaker Rayburn, fellow Democrats, I want to express my thanks to Governor Stevenson for his generous and heart-warming introduction.

It was my great honor to place his name in nomination at the 1956 Democratic Convention, and I am delighted to have his support and his counsel and his advice in the coming months ahead.

With a deep sense of duty and high resolve, I accept your nomination.

I accept it with a full and grateful heart—without reservation—and with only one obligation—the obligation to devote every effort of body, mind and spirit to lead our Party back to victory and our Nation back to greatness.

I am grateful, too, that you have provided me with such an eloquent statement of our Party's platform. Pledges which are made so eloquently are made to be kept. "The Rights of Man"—the civil and economic rights essential to the human dignity of all men—are indeed our goal and our first principles. This is a platform on which I can run with enthusiasm and conviction.

And I am grateful, finally, that I can rely in the coming months on so many others—on a distinguished running-mate who brings unity to our ticket and strength to our platform, Lyndon Johnson—on one of the most articulate statesmen of our time, Adlai Stevenson—on a great spokesman for our needs as a Nation and a people, Stuart Symington—and on that fighting campaigner whose support I welcome, President Harry S. Truman—on my traveling companion in Wisconsin and West Virginia, Senator Hubert Humphrey. On Paul Butler, our devoted and courageous Chairman.

I feel a lot safer now that they are on my side again. And I am proud of the contrast with our Republican competitors. For their ranks are apparently so thin that not one challenger has come forth with both the competence and the courage to make theirs an open convention.

I am fully aware of the fact that the Democratic Party, by nominating someone of my faith, has taken on what many regard as a new and hazardous risk—new, at least since 1928. But I look at it this way: the Democratic Party has once again placed its confidence in the American people, and in their ability to render a free, fair judgment. And you have, at the same time, placed your confidence in me, and in my ability to render a free, fair judgment—to uphold the Constitution and my oath of office—and to reject any kind of religious pressure or obligation that might directly or indirectly interfere with my conduct of the Presidency in the national interest. My record of fourteen years supporting public education—supporting complete separation of church and state—and resisting pressure from any source on any issue should be clear by now to everyone.

I hope that no American, considering the really critical issues facing this country, will waste his franchise by voting either for me or against me solely on account of my religious affiliation. It is not relevant. I want to stress what some other political or religious leader may have said on this subject. It is not relevant what abuses may have existed in other countries or in other times. It is not relevant what pressures, if any, might conceivably be brought to bear on me. I am telling you now what you are entitled to know: that my decisions on any public policy will be my own—as an American, a Democrat, and a free man.

Under any circumstances, however, the victory we seek in November will not be easy. We all know that in our hearts. We recognize the power of the forces that will be aligned against us. We know they will invoke the name of Abraham Lincoln on behalf of their candidate—despite the fact that the political career of their candidate has often seemed to show charity toward none and malice for all.

We know that it will not be easy to campaign against a man who has

Paperweight with PT 109 design, given to Kennedy delegates at the 1960 Democratic convention.

In the fall of 1941, John Kennedy joined the U.S. Navy and two years later was sent to the South Pacific. He barely escaped death in battle. Commanding a patrol torpedo (PT) boat, he was severely injured when a Japanese destroyer sank it in the Solomon Islands. Marooned far behind enemy lines, he led his men back to safety. He was awarded the U.S. Navy and Marine Corps medal for heroism. These events were later depicted in a major Hollywood film, *PT 109*, that contributed to the Kennedy mystique.

spoken or voted on every known side of every known issue. Mr. Nixon may feel it is his turn now, after the New Deal and the Fair Deal—but before he deals, someone had better cut the cards.

That "someone" may be the millions of Americans who voted for President Eisenhower but balk at his would be, self-appointed successor. For just as historians tell us that Richard I was not fit to fill the shoes of bold Henry II—and that Richard Cromwell was not fit to wear the mantle of his uncle—they might add in future years that Richard Nixon did not measure to the footsteps of Dwight D. Eisenhower.

Perhaps he could carry on the party policies—the policies of Nixon, Benson, Dirksen, and Goldwater. But this Nation cannot afford such a luxury. Perhaps we could better afford a Coolidge following Harding. And perhaps we could afford a Pierce following Fillmore. But after Buchanan this nation needed a Lincoln—after Taft we needed a Wilson—after Hoover we needed Franklin Roosevelt. . . . And after eight years of drugged and fitful sleep, this nation needs strong, creative Democratic leadership in the White House.

But we are not merely running against Mr. Nixon. Our task is not merely one of itemizing Republican failures. Nor is that wholly necessary. For the families forced from the farm will know how to vote without our telling them. The unemployed miners and textile workers will know how to vote. The old people without medical care—the families without a decent home—the parents of children without adequate food or schools—they all know that it's time for a change.

But I think the American people expect more from us than cries of indignation and attack. The times are too grave, the challenge too urgent, and the stakes too high to permit the customary passions of political debate. We are not here to curse the darkness, but to light the candle that can guide us through that darkness to a safe and sane future. As Winston Churchill said on taking office some twenty years ago: if we open a quarrel between the present and the past, we shall be in danger of losing the future.

Today our concern must be with that future. For the world is changing. The old era is ending. The old ways will not do.

Abroad, the balance of power is shifting. There are new and more terrible weapons—new and uncertain nations—new pressures of population and deprivation. One-third of the world, it has been said, may be free—but one-third is the victim of cruel repression—and the other one-third is rocked by the pangs of poverty, hunger and envy. More energy is released by the awakening of these new nations than by the fission of the atom itself.

Meanwhile, Communist influence has penetrated further into Asia, stood astride the Middle East and now festers some ninety miles off the coast of Florida. Friends have slipped into neutrality—and neutrals into hostility. As our keynoter reminded us, the President who began his career by going to Korea ends it by staying away from Japan.

The world has been close to war before—but now man, who has survived all previous threats to his existence, has taken into his mortal hands the power to exterminate the entire species some seven times over.

Here at home, the changing face of the future is equally revolutionary. The

Kennedy had won election to the House of Representatives from Massachusetts in 1946 and to the Senate in 1952 on his good looks, his father's wealth, and his World War II record. Although he remained an outsider in Congress, he had come within a few votes of winning the vice presidential nomination at the 1956 Democratic convention. At that time, Kennedy set his sights on the 1960 election. He criss-crossed the country several times, meeting local politicians and charming audiences. After being reelected to the Senate in 1958, Kennedy and his family began to put together a very efficient national political organization. He emerged as the leading Democratic candidate after primary

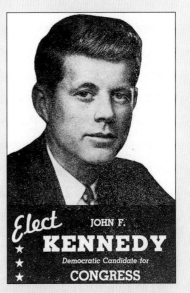

victories in New Hampshire, Wisconsin, and West Virginia over Senator Hubert Humphrey of Minnesota. At the Los Angeles convention, Kennedy won the nomination on the first ballot. He offered the vice presidential spot to Senator Lyndon Johnson of Texas and Johnson accepted. This decision would shape U.S. presidential politics for the rest of the decade.

(Top right) postcard from John Kennedy's Massachusetts Democratic congressional primary, June 18, 1946; (bottom left) celluloid button promoting Kennedy for the 1956 vice presidential nomination. In 1957, Kennedy received the Pulitzer Prize for his book *Profiles in Courage*, a study of senators who risked their careers for what they regarded to be right; (bottom right) poster from Kennedy's 1958 Massachusetts senatorial campaign.

New Deal and the Fair Deal were bold measures for their generations—but this is a new generation.

A technological revolution on the farm has led to an output explosion—but we have not yet learned to harness that explosion usefully, while protecting our farmers' right to full parity income.

An urban population explosion has overcrowded our schools, cluttered up our suburbs, and increased the squalor of our slums.

A peaceful revolution for human rights—demanding an end to racial discrimination in all parts of our community life—has strained at the leashes imposed by timid executive leadership.

A medical revolution has extended the life of our elder citizens without providing the dignity and security those later years deserve. And a revolution of automation finds machines replacing men in the mines and mills of America, without replacing their incomes or their training or their needs to pay the family doctor, grocer and landlord.

There has also been a change—a slippage—in our intellectual and moral strength. Seven lean years of drought and famine have withered a field of ideas. Blight has descended on our regulatory agencies—and a dry rot, beginning in Washington, is seeping into every corner of America—in the payola mentality, the expense account way of life, the confusion between what is legal and what is right. Too many Americans have lost their way, their will and their sense of historic purpose.

It is a time, in short, for a new generation of leadership—new men to cope with new problems and new opportunities.

All over the world, particularly in the newer nations, young men are coming to power—men who are not bound by the traditions of the past—men who are not blinded by the old fears and hates and rivalries—young men who can cast off the old slogans and delusions and suspicions.

The Republican nominee-to-be, of course, is also a young man. But his approach is as old as McKinley. His party is the party of the past. His speeches are generalities from Poor Richard's Almanac. Their platform, made up of left-over Democratic planks, has the courage of our old convictions. Their pledge is a pledge to the status quo—and today there can be no status quo.

For I stand tonight facing west on what was once the last frontier. From the lands that stretch three thousand miles behind me, the pioneers of old gave up their safety, their comfort and sometimes their lives to build a new world here in the West. They were not the captives of their own doubts, the prisoners of their own price tags. Their motto was not "every man for himself"—but "all for the common cause." They were determined to make that new world strong and free, to overcome its hazards and its hardships, to conquer the enemies that threatened from without and within.

Today some would say that those struggles are all over—that all the horizons have been explored—that all the battles have been won—that there is no longer an American frontier.

But I trust that no one in this vast assemblage will agree with those sentiments. For the problems are not all solved and the battles are not all won—and we stand today on the edge of a New Frontier—the frontier of the 1960s—a frontier of unknown opportunities and perils—a frontier of unfulfilled hopes and threats.

Woodrow Wilson's New Freedom promised our nation a new political and economic framework. Franklin Roosevelt's New Deal promised security and succor to those in need. But the New Frontier of which I speak is not a set of promises—it is a set of challenges. It sums up not what I intend to offer the American people, but what I intend to ask of them. It appeals to their pride, not to their pocketbook—it holds out the promise of more sacrifice instead of more security.

But I tell you the New Frontier is here, whether we seek it or not. Beyond that frontier are the uncharted areas of science and space, unsolved problems of peace and war, unconquered pockets of ignorance and prejudice, unanswered questions of poverty and surplus. It would be easier to shrink back from that frontier, to look to the safe mediocrity of the past, to be lulled by good intentions and high rhetoric—and those who prefer that course should not cast their votes for me, regardless of party.

But I believe the times demand new invention, innovation, imagination, decision. I am asking each of you to be pioneers on that New Frontier. My call is to the young in heart, regardless of age—to all who respond to the Scriptural call: "Be strong and of a good courage; be not afraid, neither be thou dismayed."

For courage—not complacency—is our need today—leadership—not salesmanship. And the only valid test of leadership is the ability to lead, and lead vigorously. A tired nation, said David Lloyd George, is a Tory nation—and the United States today cannot afford to be either tired or Tory.

There may be those who wish to hear more—more promises to this group or that—more harsh rhetoric about the men in the Kremlin—more assurances of a golden future, where taxes are always low and subsidies ever high. But my promises are in the platform you have adopted—our ends will not be won by rhetoric and we can have faith in the future only if we have faith in ourselves.

For the harsh facts of the matter are that we stand on this frontier at a turning-point in history. We must prove all over again whether this nation—or any nation so conceived—can long endure—whether our society—with its freedom of choice, its breadth of opportunity, its range of alternatives—can compete with the single-minded advance of the Communist system.

Can a nation organized and governed such as ours endure? That is the real question. Have we the nerve and the will? Can we carry through in an age where we will witness not only new breakthroughs in weapons of destruction—but also a race for mastery of the sky and the rain, the ocean and the tides, the far side of space and the inside of men's minds?

Are we up to the task—are we equal to the challenge? Are we willing to match the Russian sacrifice of the present for the future—or must we sacrifice our future in order to enjoy the present?

That is the question of the New Frontier. That is the choice our nation must make—a choice that lies not merely between two men or two parties, but between the public interest and private comfort—between national greatness and national decline—between the fresh air of progress and the stale, dank atmosphere of "normalcy"—between determined dedication and creeping mediocrity.

All mankind waits upon our decision. A whole world looks to see what we will do. We cannot fail their trust, we cannot fail to try.

It has been a long road from that first snowy day in New Hampshire to this crowded convention city. Now begins another long journey, taking me into your cities and homes all over America. Give me your help, your hand, your voice, your vote. Recall with me the words of Isaiah: "They that wait upon the Lord shall renew their strength; they shall mount up with wings as eagles; they shall run and not be weary."

As we face the coming challenge, we too, shall wait upon the Lord, and ask that he renew our strength. Then shall we be equal to the test. Then we shall not be weary. And then we shall prevail.

★ Excerpt from the First Debate ★

The 1960 presidential campaign was memorable for an unprecedented series of four debates between the two candidates over all major television and radio networks at prime viewing time in late September and October. To the surprise of both his advisors and his adversaries, a confident Nixon accepted Kennedy's challenge. Thus, the largest television audience in American history up to then—estimated at 70 million adults—watched the candidates confront each other. Although Nixon performed well rhetorically, Kennedy managed to portray an appealing image of youthfulness, energy, and physical poise, which convinced many that he had won the debates. Kennedy, rested and well briefed, seemed forceful and at ease in answering questions posed by a panel of newsmen. Nixon looked pale and tired and seemed hesitant and defensive. In retrospect, it seems that Nixon never recovered from the negative effects of the first debate, in which Kennedy's articulate presentation succeeded in elevating him to the vice president's level—and this even matching in the popular imagination was for Kennedy a major victory.

HOWARD K. SMITH, moderator: Good evening. The television and radio stations of the United States and their affiliated stations are proud to provide facilities for a discussion of issues in the current political campaign by the two major candidates for the presidency. The candidates need no introduction. The Republican candidate, Vice President Richard M. Nixon, and the Democratic candidate, Senator John F. Kennedy. According to rules set by the candidates themselves, each man shall make an opening statement of approximately eight minutes' duration and a closing statement of approximately three minutes' duration. In between the candidates will answer, or comment upon answers to questions put by a panel of correspondents. In this, the first discussion in a series of four joint appearances, the subject matter, it has been agreed, will be restricted to internal or domestic American matters. And now for the first opening statement by Senator John F. Kennedy.

Senator KENNEDY: Mr. Smith, Mr. Nixon. In the election of 1860, Abraham Lincoln said the question was whether this nation could exist half-slave or half-free. In the election of 1960, and with the world around us, the question is whether the world will exist half-slave or half-free, whether it will move in the direction of freedom, in the direction of the road that we are taking, or whether it will move in the direction of slavery. I think it will depend in great measure upon what we do here in the United States, on the kind of society that we build, on the kind of strength that we maintain. We discuss tonight domestic issues, but I would not want that to be any implication to be given that this does not involve directly our struggle with Mr. Khrushchev for survival. Mr. Khrushchev is in New York, and he maintains the Communist offensive throughout the world because of the productive power of the Soviet Union itself. The Chinese Communists have always had a large population. But they are important and dangerous now because they are mounting a major effort within their own country. The kind of country we have here, the kind of society we have, the kind of strength we build in the United States will be the defense of freedom. If we do well here, if we meet our obligations, if we're moving ahead, then I think freedom will be secure around the world. If we fail, then freedom fails. Therefore, I think the question before the American people is: Are we doing as much as we can do? Are we as strong as we should be? Are we as strong as we must be if we're going to maintain our independence, and if we're going to maintain and hold out the hand of friendship to those who look to us for assistance, to those who look to us for survival? I should make it very clear that I do not think we're doing enough, that I am not satisfied as an American with the progress that we're making. This is a great country, but I think it could be a greater country; and this is a powerful country, but I think it could be a more powerful country. I'm not satisfied to have 50 percent of our steel-mill capacity unused. I'm not satisfied when the United States had last year the lowest rate of economic growth of any major industrialized society in the world. Because economic growth means strength and vitality; it means we're able to sustain our defenses; it means we're able to meet our commitments abroad. I'm not satisfied when we have over $9 billion worth of food—some of it rotting—even though there is a hungry world, and even though four million Americans wait every month for a food package from the government, which averages five cents a day per individual. I saw cases in West Virginia, here in the United States, where children took home part of their school lunch in order to feed their families because I don't think we're meeting our obligations toward these Americans. I'm not satisfied when the Soviet Union is turning out twice as many scientists and engineers as we are. I'm not satisfied when many of our teachers are inadequately paid, or when our children go to school on part-time shifts. I think we should have an educational system second to none. I'm not satisfied when I see men like Jimmy Hoffa—in charge of the largest union in the United States—still free. I'm not satisfied when we are failing to develop the natural resources of the

United States to the fullest. Here in the United States, which developed the Tennessee Valley and which built the Grand Coulee and the other dams in the Northwest United States at the present rate of hydropower production—and that is the hallmark of an industrialized society—the Soviet Union by 1975 will be producing more power than we are. These are all the things, I think, in this country that can make our society strong, or can mean that it stands still. I'm not satisfied until every American enjoys his full constitutional rights. If a Negro baby is born—and this is true also of Puerto Ricans and Mexicans in some of our cities—he has about one-half as much chance to get through high school as a white baby. He has one-third as much chance to get through college as a white student. He has about a third as much chance to be a professional man, about half as much chance to own a house. He has about four times as much chance that he'll be out of work in his life as the white baby. I think we can do better. I don't want the talents of any American to go to waste. I know that there are those who say that we want to turn everything over to the government. I don't at all. I want the individuals to meet their responsibilities. And I want the states to meet their responsibilities. But I think there is also a national responsibility. The argument has been used against every piece of social legislation in the last twenty-five years. The people of the United States individually could not have developed the Tennessee Valley; collectively they could have. A cotton farmer in Georgia or a peanut farmer or a dairy farmer in Wisconsin and Minnesota, he cannot protect himself against the forces of supply and demand in the market place; but working together in effective governmental programs he can do so. Seventeen million Americans, who live over sixty-five on an average Social Security check of about $78 a month, they're not able to sustain themselves individually, but they can sustain themselves through the social security system. I don't believe in big government, but I believe in effective governmental action. And I think that's the only way that the United States is going to maintain its freedom. It's the only way that we're going to move ahead. I think we can do a better job. I think we're going to have to do a better job if we are going to meet the responsibilities which time and events have placed upon us. We cannot turn the job over to anyone else. If the United States fails, then the whole cause of freedom fails. And I think it depends in great measure on what we do here in this country. The reason Franklin Roosevelt was a good neighbor in Latin America was because he was a good neighbor in the United States. Because they felt that the American society was moving again. I want us to recapture that image. I want people in Latin America and Africa and Asia to start to look to America; to see how we're doing things; to wonder what the president of the United States is doing; and not to look at Khrushchev, or look at the Chinese Communists. That is the obligation upon our generation. In 1933, Franklin Roosevelt said in his inaugural that his generation of Americans has a rendezvous with destiny. I think our generation of Americans has the same rendezvous. The question now is: Can freedom be maintained under the most severe attack it has ever known? I think it can be. And I think in the final analysis it depends upon what we do here. I think it's time America started moving again.

Mr. SMITH: And now the opening statement by Vice President Richard M. Nixon.

Mr. NIXON: Mr. Smith, Senator Kennedy. The things that Senator Kennedy has said many of us can agree with. There is no question but that we cannot discuss our internal affairs in the United States without recognizing that they have a tremendous bearing on our international position. There is no question but that this nation cannot stand still; because we are in a deadly competition. a competition not only with the men in the Kremlin, but the men in Peking. We're ahead in this competition, as Senator Kennedy, I think, has implied. But when you're in a race, the only way to stay ahead is to move ahead. And I subscribe completely to the spirit that Senator Kennedy has expressed tonight, the spirit that the United States should move ahead. Where, then, do we disagree? I think we disagree on the implication of his remarks tonight and on the statements that he has made on many occasions during his campaign to the effect that the United States has been standing still. We heard tonight, for example, the statement made that our growth in national product last year was the lowest of any industrial nation in the world. Now last year, of course, was 1958. That happened to be a recession year. But when we look at the growth of G.N.P. this year, a year of recovery, we find that it's 6-$^9/_{10}$ percent and one of the highest in the world today. More about that later. Looking then to this problem of how the United States should move ahead and where the United States is moving, I think it is well that we take the advice of a very famous campaigner: Let's look at the record. Is the United States standing still? Is it true that this administration, as Senator Kennedy has charged, has been an administration of retreat, of defeat, of stagnation? Is it true that, as far as this country is concerned, in the field of electric power, in all of the fields that he has mentioned, we have not been moving ahead? Well, we have a comparison that we can make. We have the record of the Truman Administration of seven-and-a-half years and the seven-and-a-half years of the Eisenhower Administration. When we compare these two records in the areas that Senator Kennedy has discussed tonight, I think we find that America has been moving ahead. Let's take schools. We have built more schools in these last seven-and-a-half years than we built in the previous seven and a half—for that matter in the last twenty years. Let's take hydroelectric power. We have developed more hydroelectric power in these seven-and-a-half years than was developed in any previous administration in history. Let us take hospitals. We find that more have been built in this administration than in the previous administration. The same is true of highways. Let's put it in terms that all of us can understand. We often hear gross national product discussed and in that respect may I say that when we compare the growth in this administration with that of the previous administration that then there was a total growth of 11 percent over seven years; in this administration there has been a total growth of 19 percent over seven years. That shows that there's been more growth in this administration than in its predecessor. But let's not put it there; let's put it in terms of the average family. What has happened to you? We find that your wages have gone up five times as much in the Eisenhower Administration as they did in the Truman Administration. What about the prices you pay? We find that the prices you pay went up five times as much in the Truman Administration as they did in the Eisenhower Administration. What's the net result of this? This means that the average family income went up 15 percent in the Eisenhower years as against 2 percent in the Truman years. Now, this is not standing still. But, good as this record is, may I emphasize it isn't enough. A record is never something to stand on. It's something to build on. And in building on this record, I believe that we have the secret for progress, we know the way to progress. And I think, first of all, our own record proves that we know the way. Senator Kennedy has suggested that he believes he knows the way. I respect the sincerity with which he makes that suggestion. But on the other hand, when we look at the various programs that he offers, they do not seem to be new. They seem to be simply retreads of the programs of the Truman Administration which preceded it. And I would suggest that during the course of the evening he might indicate those areas in which his programs are new, where they will mean more progress than we had then. What kind of programs are we for? We are for programs that will expand educational opportunities, that will give to all Americans their equal chance for education, for all of the things which are necessary and dear to the hearts of our people. We are for programs, in addition, which will see that our medical care for the aged is much better handled than it is at the present time. Here again, may I indicate that Senator Kennedy and I are not in disagreement as to the aims. We both want to help the old people. We want to see that they do have adequate medical care. The question is the means. I think that the means that I advocate will reach that goal better than the means that he advocates. I could give better examples, but for whatever it is, whether it's in the field of housing, or health, or medical care, or schools, or the development of electric power, we have programs which we believe will move America, move her forward and build on the wonderful record that we have made over these past seven-and-a-half years. Now, when we look at these programs, might I suggest that in evaluating them we often have a tendency to say that the test of a program is how much you're spending. I will concede that in all the areas to which I have referred Senator Kennedy would have the federal government spend more than I would have it spend. I costed out the cost of the Democratic platform. It runs a minimum of $13.2 billion a year more than we are presently spending to a maximum of $18 billion a year more than we're presently spending. Now the Republican platform will cost more too. It will cost a minimum of $4 billion a year more, a maximum of $4.9 billion a year more than we're presently spending. Now, does this mean that his program is better than ours? Not at all. Because it isn't a question of how much the federal government spends; it isn't a question of which government does the most. It's a question of which administration does the right thing. And in our case, I do believe that our programs will stimulate the creative energies of 180 million free Americans. I believe the programs that Senator Kennedy advocates will have a tendency to stifle those creative energies. I believe, in other words, that his program would lead to the stagnation of the motive power that we need in this country to get progress. The final point that I would like to make is this: Senator Kennedy has suggested in his speeches that we lack compassion for the poor, for the old, and for others that are unfortunate. Let us understand throughout this campaign that his motives and mine are sincere. I know what it means to be poor. I know what it means to see people who are unemployed. I know Senator Kennedy feels as deeply about these problems as I do, but our disagreement is not about the goals for America but only about the means to reach those goals.

Mr. SMITH: Thank you, Mr. Nixon. That completes the opening statements, and now the candidates will answer questions or comment upon one another's answers to questions, put by correspondents of the networks.

Bob FLEMING, ABC News: Senator, the vice president in his campaign has said that you were naive and at times immature. He has raised the question of leadership. On this issue, why do you think people should vote for you rather than the vice president?

Mr. KENNEDY: Well, the vice president and I came to the Congress together in 1946; we both served in the Labor Committee. I've been there now 14 years, the same period of time that he has, so that our experience in government is comparable. Secondly, I think the question is what are the programs that we advocate, what is the party record that we lead? I come out of the Democratic Party, which in this century has produced Woodrow Wilson and Franklin Roosevelt and Harry Truman, and which supported and sustained these programs which I've discussed tonight. Mr. Nixon comes out of the Republican Party. He was nominated by it. And it is a fact that through most of these last 25 years the Republican leadership has opposed federal aid for education, medical care for the aged, development of the Tennessee Valley, development of our natural resources. I think Mr. Nixon is an effective leader of his party. I hope he would grant me the same. The question before us is: which point of view and which party do we want to lead the United States?

Mr. SMITH: Mr. Nixon, would you like to comment on that statement?

Mr. NIXON: I have no comment. [. . .]

Mr. Stuart NOVINS, CBS News: Mr. Vice President, your campaign stresses the value of your eight-year experience, and the question arises as to whether that experience was as an observer or as a participant or as an initiator of policy-making. Would you tell us please specifically what major proposals you have made in the last eight years that have been adopted by the administration?

Mr. NIXON: It would be rather difficult to cover them in two-and-a-half minutes. I would suggest that these proposals could be mentioned. First, after each of my foreign trips I have made recommendations that have been adopted.

For example, after my first trip abroad, I strongly recommended that we increase our exchange programs particularly as they related to exchange of persons and of leaders in the labor field and in the information field. After my trip to South America, I made recommendations that a separate inter-American lending agency be set up which the South American nations would like much better than to participate in the lending agencies which treated all the countries of the world the same. I have made other recommendations after each of the other trips; for example, after my trip abroad to Hungary I made some recommendations with regard to the Hungarian refugee situation which were adopted, not only by the president but some of them were enacted into law by the Congress. Within the administration, as a chairman of the President's Committee on Price Stability and Economic Growth, I have had the opportunity to make recommendations which have been adopted within the administration and which I think have been reasonably effective. I know Senator Kennedy suggested in his speech at Cleveland yesterday that that committee had not been particularly effective. I would only suggest that while we do not take the credit for it—I would not presume to—that since that committee has been formed the price line has been held very well within the United States.

Mr. KENNEDY: That's what I found somewhat unsatisfactory about the figures, Mr. Nixon, that you used in your previous speech, when you talked about the Truman Administration. Mr. Truman came to office in 1944 and at the end of the war, and difficulties that were facing the United States during that period of transition—1946 when price controls were lifted—so it's rather difficult to use an over-all figure taking those seven-and-a-half years and comparing them to the last eight years. I prefer to take the overall percentage record of the last 20 years of the Democrats and the eight years of the Republicans to show an overall period of growth. In regard to price stability I'm not aware that that committee did produce recommendations that ever were certainly before the Congress from the point of view of legislation in regard to controlling prices. In regard to the exchange of students and labor unions, I am chairman of the subcommittee on Africa and I think that one of the most unfortunate phases of our policy towards that country was the very minute number of exchanges that we had. I think it's true of Latin America also. We did come forward with a program of students for the Congo of over 300 which was more than the federal government had for all of Africa the previous year, so that I don't think that we have moved, at least in those areas, with sufficient vigor. [. . .]

Mr. Charles WARREN, Mutual News: Senator Kennedy, during your brief speech a few minutes ago you mentioned farm surpluses.

Mr. KENNEDY: That's correct.

Mr. WARREN: I'd like to ask this: It's a fact, I think, that presidential candidates traditionally make promises to farmers. Lots of people, I think, don't understand why the government pays farmers for not producing certain crops—or paying farmers if they overproduce for that matter. Now, let me ask, sir, why can't the farmer operate like the business man who operates a factory? If an auto company overproduces a certain model car Uncle Sam doesn't step in and buy up the surplus. Why this constant courting of the farmer?

Mr. KENNEDY: Well, because I think that if the federal government moved out of the program and withdrew its supports then I think you would have complete economic chaos. The farmer plants in the spring and harvests in the fall. There are hundreds of thousands of them. They really are not able to control their market very well. They bring their crops in or their livestock in, many of them about the same time. They have only a few purchasers that buy their milk or their hogs—a few large companies in many cases—and therefore the farmer is not in a position to bargain very effectively in the market place. I think the experience of the twenties has shown what a free market could do to agriculture. And if the agricultural economy collapses, then the economy of the rest of the United States sooner or later will collapse. The farmers are the number one market for the automobile industry of the United

States. The automobile industry is the number one market for steel. So if the farmers' economy continues to decline as sharply as it has in recent years, then I think you would have a recession in the rest of the country. So I think the case for the government intervention is a good one. Secondly, my objection to present farm policy is that there are no effective controls to bring supply and demand into better balance. The dropping of the support price in order to limit production does not work, and we now have the highest surpluses—$9 billion worth. We've had a higher tax load from the Treasury for the farmer in the last few years with the lowest farm income in many years. I think that this farm policy has failed. In my judgment the only policy that will work will be for effective supply and demand to be in balance. And that can only be done through governmental action. I therefore suggest that in those basic commodities which are supported, that the federal government, after endorsement by the farmers in that commodity, attempt to bring supply and demand into balance—attempt effective production controls—so that we won't have that 5 or 6 percent surplus which breaks the price 15 or 20 percent. I think Mr. Benson's program has failed. And I must say, after reading the vice president's speech before the farmers, as he read mine, I don't believe that it's very different from Mr. Benson's. I don't think it provides effective governmental controls. I think the support prices are tied to the average market price of the last three years, which was Mr. Benson's theory. I therefore do not believe that this is a sharp enough breach with the past to give us any hope of success for the future.

Mr. SMITH: Mr. Nixon, comment?

Mr. NIXON: I of course disagree with Senator Kennedy insofar as his suggestions as to what should be done on the farm program. He has made the suggestion that what we need is to move in the direction of more government controls, a suggestion that would also mean raising prices that the consumers pay for products and imposing upon the farmers controls on acreage even far more than they have today. I think this is the wrong direction. I don't think this has worked in the past; I do not think it will work in the future. The program that I have advocated is one which departs from the present program that we have in this respect. It recognizes that the government has a responsibility to get the farmer out of the trouble he presently is in because the government got him into it. And that's the fundamental reason why he can't let the farmer go by himself at the present time. The farmer produced these surpluses because the government asked him to through legislation during the war. Now that we have these surpluses, it's our responsibility to indemnify the farmer during that period that we get rid of the farmer—the surpluses. Until we get the surpluses off the farmer's back, however, we should have a program such as I announced, which will see that farm income holds up. But I would propose holding that income up not through a type of program that Senator Kennedy has suggested that would raise prices, but one that would indemnify the farmer, pay the farmer in kind from the products which are in surplus.

Mr. SMITH: The next question to Vice President Nixon from Mr. Vanocur.

Mr. Sander VANOCUR, NBC News: Mr. Vice President, since the question of executive leadership is a very important campaign issue, I'd like to follow Mr. Novin's question. Now, Republican campaign slogans—you'll see them on signs around the country as you did last week—say it's experience that counts—that's over a picture of yourself, sir, implying that you've had more governmental executive decision-making experience than your opponent. Now, in his news conference on August 24, President Eisenhower was asked to give one example of a major idea of yours that he adopted. His reply was, and I'm quoting: "If you give me a week I might think of one. I don't remember." Now that was a month ago, sir, and the president hasn't brought it up since, and I'm wondering, sir, if you can clarify which version is correct— the one put out by Republican campaign leaders or the one put out by President Eisenhower?

Mr. NIXON: Well, I would suggest, Mr. Vanocur, that if you know the president, that was probably a facetious remark. I would also suggest that insofar as his statement is concerned, that I think it would be improper for the president of the United States to disclose the instances in which members of his official family had made recommendations, as I have made them through the years to him, which he has accepted or rejected. The president has always maintained and very properly so that he is entitled to get what advice he wants from his cabinet and from his other advisers without disclosing that to anybody—including as a matter of fact the Congress. Now, I can only say this. Through the years I have sat in the National Security Council. I have been in the cabinet. I have met with the legislative leaders. I have met with the president when he made the great decisions with regard to Lebanon, Quemoy and Matsu, other matters. The president has asked for my advice. I have given it. Sometimes my advice has been taken. Sometimes it has not. I do not say that I have made the decisions. And I would say that no president should ever allow anybody else to make the major decisions. The president only makes the decisions. All that his advisers do is to give counsel when he asks for it. As far as what experience counts and whether that is experience that counts, that isn't for me to say. I can only say that my experience is there for the people to consider; Senator Kennedy's is there for the people to consider. As he pointed out, we came to the Congress in the same year. His experience has been different from mine. Mine has been in the executive branch. His has been in the legislative branch. I would say that the people now have the opportunity to evaluate his as against mine and I think both he and I are going to abide by whatever the people decide.

Mr. SMITH: Senator Kennedy.

Mr. KENNEDY: Well, I'll just say that the question is of experience—and the question also is what our judgment is of the future, and what our goals are for the United States, and what ability we have to implement those goals. Abraham Lincoln came to the presidency in 1860 after a rather little known session in the House of Representatives and after being defeated for the

Senate in fifty-eight and was a distinguished president. There's no certain road to the presidency. There are no guarantees that if you take one road or another that you will be a successful president. I have been in the Congress for fourteen years. I have voted in the [Senate for the] last eight years and the vice president was presiding over the Senate and meeting his other responsibilities. I have made decisions over 800 times on matters which affect not only the domestic security of the United States, but as a member of the Senate Foreign Relations Committee. The question really is: which candidate and which party can meet the problems that the United States is going to face in the sixties?

Mr. SMITH: The next question to Senator Kennedy from Mr. Novins.

Mr. NOVINS: Senator Kennedy, in connection with these problems of the future that you speak of, and the program that you enunciated earlier in your direct talk, you call for expanding some of the welfare programs for schools, for teacher salaries, medical care, and so forth; but you also call for reducing the federal debt. And I'm wondering how you, if you're president in January, would go about paying the bill for all this. Does this mean that you—

Mr. KENNEDY: I didn't indicate—I did not advocate reducing the federal debt because I don't believe that you're going to be able to reduce the federal debt very much in 1961, '62, or '63. I think you have heavy obligations which affect our security, which we're going to have to meet. And therefore I've never suggested we should be able to retire the debt substantially, or even at all in 1961 or '62.

Mr. NOVINS: Senator, I believe in one of your speeches—

Mr. KENNEDY: No, never.

Mr. NOVINS:—you suggested that reducing the interest rate would help toward—

Mr. KENNEDY: No. No. Not reducing the interest—

Mr. NOVINS:—a reduction of the Federal debt.

Mr. KENNEDY:—reducing the interest rate. In my judgment, the hard money, tight money policy, fiscal policy of this administration has contributed to the slow-down in our economy, which helped bring the recession of '54; which made the recession of '58 rather intense, and which has slowed, somewhat, our economic activity in 1960. What I have talked about, however, the kind of programs that I've talked about, in my judgment, are fiscally sound. Medical care for the aged, I would put under social security. The vice president and I disagree on this. The program—the Javits-Nixon or the Nixon-Javits program—would have cost, if fully used, $600 million by the government per year, and $600 million by the state. The program which I advocated, which failed by five votes in the United States Senate, would have put medical care for the aged in Social Security, and would have been paid for through the Social Security System and the Social Security tax. Secondly, I support federal aid to education and federal aid for teachers' salaries. I think that's a good investment. I think we're going to have to do it. And I think to heap the burden further on the property tax, which is already strained in many of our communities, will provide, will insure, in my opinion, that many of our children will not be adequately educated, and many of our teachers not adequately compensated. There is no greater return to an economy or to a society than an educational system second to none. On the question of the development of natural resources, I would pay as you go in the sense that they would be balanced and the power revenues would bring back sufficient money to finance the projects, in the same way as the Tennessee Valley. I believe in the balanced budget. And the only conditions under which I would unbalance the budget would be if there was a grave national emergency or a serious recession Otherwise, with a steady rate of economic growth—and Mr. Nixon and Mr. Rockefeller, in their meeting, said a 5 percent economic growth would bring by 1962 $10 billion extra in tax revenues. Whatever is brought in, I think that we can finance essential programs within a balanced budget, if business remains orderly.

Mr. SMITH: Mr. Nixon, your comment?

Mr. NIXON: Yes. I think what Mr. Novins was referring to was not one of Senator Kennedy's speeches, but the Democratic platform, which did mention cutting the national debt. I think, too, that it should be pointed out that of course it is not possible, particularly under the proposals that Senator Kennedy has advocated, either to cut the national debt or to reduce taxes. As a matter of fact it will be necessary to raise taxes. As Senator Kennedy points out that as far as his one proposal is concerned—the one for medical care for the aged—that that would be financed out of Social Security. That, however, is raising taxes for those who pay Social Security.

He points out that we would make pay-as-you-go be the basis for our natural resources development. Where our natural resources development— which I also support, incidentally, however—whenever you appropriate money for one of these projects, you have to pay now and appropriate the money and while they eventually do pay out, it doesn't mean that the government doesn't have to put out the money this year. And so I would say that in all of these proposals Senator Kennedy has made, they will result in one of two things: either he has to raise taxes or he has to unbalance the budget. If he unbalances the budget, that means you have inflation, and that will be, of course, a very cruel blow to the very people—the older people—that we've been talking about. As far as aid for school construction is concerned, I favor that, as Senator Kennedy did, in January of this year, when he said he favored that rather than aid to teacher salaries. I favor that because I believe that's the best way to aid our schools without running any risk whatever of the federal government telling our teachers what to teach.

Mr. SMITH: The next question to Vice President Nixon from Mr. Warren.

Mr. WARREN: Mr. Vice President you mentioned schools and it was just yesterday I think you asked for a crash program to raise education standards, and this evening you talked about advances in education. Mr. Vice President, you said—it was back in 1957—that salaries paid to school teachers were nothing short of a national disgrace. Higher salaries for teachers, you added, were important and if the situation wasn't corrected it could lead to a national disaster. And yet, you refused to vote in the Senate in order to break a tie vote when that single vote, if it had been yes, would have granted salary increases to teachers. I wonder if you could explain that, sir.

Mr. NIXON: I'm awfully glad you got that question because as you know I got into it at the last of my other question and wasn't able to complete the argument. I think that the reason that I voted against having the federal government pay teachers' salaries was probably the very reason that concerned Senator Kennedy when in January of this year, in his kick-off press conference, he said that he favored aid for school construction, but at that time did not feel that there should be aid for teachers' salaries—at least that's the way I read his remarks. Now, why should there be any question about the federal government aiding teachers' salaries? Why did Senator Kennedy take that position then? Why do I take it now? We both took it then, and I take it now, for this reason: we want higher teachers' salaries. We need higher teachers' salaries. But we also want our education to be free of federal control. When the federal government gets the power to pay teachers, inevitably in my opinion, it will acquire the power to set standards and to tell the teachers what to teach. I think this would be bad for the country; I think it would be bad for the teaching profession. There is another point that should be made. I favor higher salaries for teachers. But, as Senator Kennedy said in January of this year in this same press conference, the way that you get higher salaries for teachers is to support school construction, which means that all of the local school districts in the various states then have money which is freed to raise the standards for teachers' salaries. I should also point out this: once you put the responsibility on the federal government for paying a portion of teachers' salaries, your local communities and your states are not going to meet the responsibility as much as they should. I believe, in other words, that we have seen the local communities and the state assuming more of that responsibility. Teachers' salaries very fortunately have gone up 50 percent in the last eight

KENNEDY-JOHNSO

two great Democrat

Poster for Kennedy and Johnson.

years as against only a 34 percent rise for other salaries. This is not enough; it should be more. But I do not believe that the way to get more salaries for teachers is to have the federal government get in with a massive program. My objection here is not the cost in dollars. My objection here is the potential cost in controls and eventual freedom for the American people by giving the federal government power over education, and that is the greatest power a government can have.

Mr. SMITH: Senator Kennedy's comment?

Mr. KENNEDY: When the Vice President quotes me in January 1960, I do not believe the federal government should pay directly teachers' salaries, but that was not the issue before the Senate in February. The issue before the Senate was that the money would be given to the state. The state then could determine whether the money should be spent for school construction or teacher salaries. On that question the Vice President and I disagreed. I voted in favor of that proposal and supported it strongly, because I think that that provided assistance to our teachers for their salaries without any chance of federal control and it is on that vote that Mr. Nixon and I disagreed, and his tie vote defeated—his breaking the tie defeated—the proposal. I don't want the federal government paying teachers' salaries directly. But if the money will go to the states and the states can then determine whether it shall go for school construction or for teachers' salaries, in my opinion you protect the local authority over the school board and the school committee. And therefore I think that was a sound proposal and that is why I supported it and I regret that it did not pass. Secondly, there have been statements made that the Democratic platform would cost a good deal of money and that I am in favor of unbalancing the budget. That is wholly wrong, wholly in error, and it is a fact that in the last eight years the Democratic Congress has reduced the requests for the appropriations by over $10 billion. That is not my view and I think it ought to be stated very clearly on the record. My view is that you can do these programs—and they should be carefully drawn—within a balanced budget if our economy is moving ahead.

Mr. SMITH: The next question to Senator Kennedy from Mr. Vanocur.

Mr. VANOCUR: Senator, you've been promising the voters that if you are elected president you'll try and push through Congress bills on medical aid to the aged, a comprehensive minimum hourly wage bill, federal aid to education. Now, in the August post-convention session of the Congress, when you at least held up the possibility you could one day be president and when you had overwhelming majorities, especially in the Senate, you could not get action on these bills. Now how do you feel that you'll be able to get them in January—

Mr. KENNEDY: Well as you take the bills—

Mr. VANOCUR:—if you weren't able to get them in August?

Mr. KENNEDY: If I may take the bills, we did pass in the Senate a bill to provide a $1.25 minimum wage. It failed because the House did not pass it and the House failed by eleven votes. And I might say that two-thirds of the Republicans in the House voted against a $1.25 minimum wage and a majority of the Democrats sustained it—nearly two-thirds of them voted for the $1.25. We were threatened by a veto if we passed a dollar and a quarter—it's extremely difficult with the great power that the president has to pass any bill when the president is opposed to it. All the president needs to sustain his veto of any bill is one-third plus one in either the House or the Senate. Secondly, we passed a federal aid to education bill in the Senate. It failed to come to the floor of the House of Representatives. It was killed in the Rules Committee. And it is a fact in the August session that the four members of the Rules Committee who were Republicans joining with two Democrats voted against sending the aid to education bill to the floor of the House. Four Democrats voted for it. Every Republican on the Rules Committee voted against sending that bill to be considered by the members of the House of Representatives. Thirdly, on medical care for the aged, this is the same fight that's been going on for twenty-five years in Social Security. We wanted to tie it to Social Security. We offered an amendment to do so. Forty-four Democrats voted for it, one Republican voted for it. And we were informed at the time it came to a vote that if it was adopted the president of the United States would veto it. In my judgment, a vigorous Democratic president supported by a Democratic majority in the House and Senate can win the support for these programs. But if you send a Republican president and a Democratic majority and the threat of a veto hangs over the Congress, in my judgment you will continue what happened in the August session, which is a clash of parties and inaction.

Mr. SMITH: Mr. Nixon, comment?

Mr. NIXON: Well obviously my views are a little different. First of all, I don't see how it's possible for a one-third of a body, such as the Republicans have in the House and the Senate to stop two-thirds, if the two-thirds are adequately led. I would say, too, that when Senator Kennedy refers to the action of the House Rules Committee, there are eight Democrats on that committee and four Republicans. It would seem to me again that it is very difficult to blame the four Republicans for the eight Democrats' not getting something through that particular committee. I would say further that to blame the president in his veto power for the inability of the Senator and his colleagues to get action in this special session misses the mark. When the president exercises his veto power, he has to have the people behind him, not just a third of the Congress. Because let's consider it. If the majority of the members of the Congress felt that these particular proposals were good issues—the majority of those who were Democrats—why didn't they pass them and send to the President and get a veto and have an issue? The reason why these particular bills in these various fields that have been mentioned were not passed was not because the President was against them; it was because the people were against them. It was because they were too extreme. And I am convinced that the alternate proposals that I have, that the Republicans have in the field of health, in the field of education, in the field of welfare, because they are not extreme, because they will accomplish the end without too great cost in dollars or in freedom, that they could get through the next Congress. [. . .]

Mr. SMITH: Mr. Warren's question for Senator Kennedy.

Mr. WARREN: Senator Kennedy, on another subject, Communism is so often described as an ideology or a belief that exists somewhere other than in the United States. Let me ask you, sir: just how serious a threat to our national security are these Communist subversive activities in the United States today?

Mr. KENNEDY: Well, I think they're serious. I think it's a matter that we should continue to give great care and attention to. We should support the laws which the United States has passed in order to protect us from those who would destroy us from within. We should sustain the Department of Justice in its efforts and the F.B.I., and we should be continually alert. I think if the United States is maintaining a strong society here in the United States, I think that we can meet any internal threat. The major threat is external and will continue.

Mr. SMITH: Mr. Nixon, comment?

Mr. NIXON: I agree with Senator Kennedy's appraisal generally in this respect. The question of Communism within the United States has been one that has worried us in the past. It is one that will continue to be a problem for years to come. We have to remember that the cold war that Mr. Khrushchev is waging and his colleagues are waging, is waged all over the world and it's waged right here in the United States. That's why we have to continue to be alert. It is also essential in being alert that we be fair; fair because by being fair we uphold the very freedoms that the Communists would destroy. We uphold the standards of conduct which they would never follow. And, in this connection, I think that we must look to the future having in mind the fact that we fight Communism at home not only by our laws to deal with Communists the few who do become Communists and the few who do become fellow travelers, but we also fight Communism at home by moving against those various injustices which exist in our society which the Communists feed upon. And in that connection I again would say that while Senator Kennedy says we are for the status quo, I do believe that he would agree that I am just as sincere in believing that my proposals for federal aid to education, my proposals for health care are just as sincerely held as his. The question again is not one of goals—we're for those goals—it's one of means.

Mr. SMITH: Mr. Vanocur's question for Vice President Nixon.

Mr. VANOCUR: Mr. Vice President in one of your earlier statements you said we've moved ahead, we've built more schools, we've built more hospitals. Now, sir, isn't it true that the building of more schools is a local matter for financing? Were you claiming that the Eisenhower Administration was responsible for the building of these schools, or is it the local school districts that provide for it?

Mr. NIXON: Not at all. As a matter of fact your question brings out a point that I'm very glad to make. Too often in appraising whether we are moving ahead or not we think only of what the federal government is doing. Now that isn't the test of whether America moves. The test of whether America moves is whether the federal government, plus the state government, plus the local government, plus the biggest segment of all—individual enterprise—moves. We have for example a gross national product of approximately $500 billion. Roughly $100 billion to $125 billion of that is the result of government activity. Four hundred billion, approximately, is a result of what individuals do. Now, the reason the Eisenhower Administration has moved, the reason that we've had the funds, for example, locally to build the schools, and the hospitals, and the highways, to make the progress that we have, is because this Administration has encouraged individual enterprise; and it has resulted in the greatest expansion of the private sector of the economy that has ever been witnessed in an eight-year period. And that is growth. That is the growth that we are looking for; it is the growth that this Administration has supported and that its policies have stimulated.

Mr. SMITH: Senator Kennedy.

Mr. KENNEDY: Well, I must say that the reason that the schools have been constructed is because the local school districts were willing to increase the property taxes to a tremendously high figure—in my opinion, almost to the point of diminishing returns in order to sustain these schools. Secondly, I think we have a rich country. And I think we have a powerful country. I think what we have to do, however, is have the president and the leadership set before our country exactly what we must do in the next decade, if we're going to maintain our security in education, in economic growth, in development of natural resources. The Soviet Union is making great gains. It isn't enough to compare what might have been done eight years ago, or ten years ago, or fifteen years ago, or twenty years ago. I want to compare what we're doing with what our adversaries are doing, so that by the year 1970 the United States is ahead in education, in health, in building, in homes, in economic strength. I think that's the big assignment, the big task, the big function of the federal government.

Mr. SMITH: Can I have the summation time please? We've completed our questions and our comments, and in just a moment, we'll have the summation time.

VOICE: This will allow three minutes and twenty seconds for the summation by each candidate.

Mr. SMITH: Three minutes and twenty seconds for each candidate. Vice President Nixon, will you make the first summation?

Mr. NIXON: Thank you, Mr. Smith, Senator Kennedy. First of all, I think it is well to put in perspective where we really do stand with regard to the Soviet Union in this whole matter of growth. The Soviet Union has been moving faster than we have. But the reason for that is obvious. They start from a much lower base. Although they have been moving faster in growth than we have, we find, for example, today that their total gross national product is only 44 percent of our total gross national product. That's the same percentage that it was twenty years ago. And as far as the absolute gap is concerned, we find that the United States is even further ahead than it was twenty years ago. Is this any reason for complacency? Not at all. Because these are determined men. They are fanatical men. And we have to get the very most out of our economy. I agree with Senator Kennedy completely on that score. Where we disagree is in the means that we would use to get the most out of our economy I respectfully submit that Senator Kennedy too often would rely too much on the federal government, on what it would do to solve our problems, to stimulate growth.

I believe that when we examine the Democratic platform, when we examine the proposals that he has discussed tonight, when we compare them with the proposals that I have made, that these proposals that he makes would not result in greater growth for this country than would be the case if we followed the programs that I have advocated There are many of the points that he has made that I would like to comment upon. The one in the field of health is worth mentioning. Our health program—the one that Senator Javits and other Republican senators, as well as I supported—is one that provides for all people over sixty-five who want health insurance, the opportunity to have it if they want it. It provides a choice of having either government insurance or private insurance. But it compels nobody to have insurance who does not want it. His program under Social Security, would require everybody who had Social Security to take government health insurance whether he wanted it or not. And it would not cover several million people who are not covered by Social Security at all. Here is one place where I think that our program does a better job than his. The other point that I would make is this: this downgrading of how much things cost I think many of our people will understand better when they look at what happened when—during the Truman Administration when the government was spending more than it took in—we found savings over a lifetime eaten up by inflation. We found the people who could least afford it—people on retired incomes—people on fixed incomes—we found them unable to meet their bills at the end of the month. It is essential that a man who's president of this country certainly stand for every program that will mean for growth. And I stand for programs that will mean growth and progress. But it is also essential that he not allow a dollar spent that could be better spent by the people themselves.

Mr. SMITH: Senator Kennedy, your conclusion.

Mr. KENNEDY: The point was made by Mr. Nixon that the Soviet production is only 44 percent of ours. I must say that 44 percent and that

Soviet country is causing us a good deal of trouble tonight. I want to make sure that it stays in that relationship. I don't want to see the day when it's 60 percent of ours, and 70 and 75 and 80 and 90 percent of ours, with all the force and power that it could bring to bear in order to cause our destruction. Secondly, the Vice President mentioned medical care for the aged. Our program was an amendment to the Kerr bill. The Kerr bill provided assistance to all those who were not on Social Security. I think it's a very clear contrast. In 1935, when the Social Security Act was written, 94 out of 95 Republicans voted against it. Mr. Landon ran in 1936 to repeal it. In August of 1960, when we tried to get it again, but this time for medical care, we received the support of one Republican in the Senate on this occasion. Thirdly, I think the question before the American people is: as they look at this country and as they look at the world around them, the goals are the same for all Americans. The means are at question. The means are at issue. If you feel that everything that is being done now is satisfactory, that the relative power and prestige and strength of the United States is increasing in relation to that of the Communists; that we've been gaining more security, that we are achieving everything as a nation that we should achieve, that we are achieving a better life for our citizens and greater strength, then I agree, I think you should vote for Mr. Nixon. But if you feel that we have to move again in the sixties, that the function of the president is to set before the people the unfinished business of our society as Franklin Roosevelt did in the thirties, the agenda for our people—what we must do as a society to meet our needs in this country and protect our security and help the cause of freedom. As I said at the beginning, the question before us all, that faces all Republicans and all Democrats is: can freedom in the next generation conquer, or are the Communists going to be successful? That's the great issue. And if we meet our responsibilities I think freedom will conquer. If we fail, if we fail to move ahead, if we fail to develop sufficient military and economic and social strength here in this country, then I think that the tide could begin to run against us. And I don't want historians, ten years from now, to say, these were the years when the tide ran out for the United States. I want them to say these were the years when the tide came in; these were the years when the United States started to move again. That's the question before the American people, and only you can decide what you want, what you want this country to be, what you want to do with the future. I think we're ready to move. And it is to that great task, if we're successful, that we will address ourselves.

Mr. SMITH: Thank you very much, gentlemen. This hour has gone by all too quickly. Thank you very much for permitting us to present the next president of the United States on this unique program. I've been asked by the candidates to thank the American networks and the affiliated stations for providing time and facilities for this joint appearance. Other debates in this series will be announced later and will be on different subjects. This is Howard K. Smith. Good night from Chicago.

Kennedy Speaks on the Religious Issue

When a group of Protestant ministers invited Senator Kennedy to discuss the question of a Catholic president, Kennedy used the opportunity to affirm that his religion, under no circumstances, would interfere with his presidential duties. The senator's forthright statement just about silenced the "religious" issue. However, on balance, Kennedy's religion did help him in Catholic districts while it hurt in the much more numerous Protestant areas. An informed estimate was that, if there had been no religious issue, Kennedy would have carried the popular vote 54 to 46 percent. (A May 1960 Gallup Poll asked: "If your party nominated a generally well-qualified man for President, and he happened to be a Catholic, would you vote for him?" Seventy-one percent responded "yes"—the current figure is 92 percent.)

Reverend Meza, Reverend Reck, I'm grateful for your generous invitation to speak my views.

While the so-called religious issue is necessarily and properly the chief topic here tonight, I want to emphasize from the outset that we have far more critical issues to face in the 1960 election; the spread of Communist influence, until it now festers 90 miles off the coast of Florida—the humiliating treatment of our president and vice president by those who no longer respect our power—the hungry children I saw in West Virginia, the old people who cannot pay their doctor bills, the families forced to give up their farms—an America with too many slums, with too few schools, and too late to the moon and outer space.

These are the real issues which should decide this campaign. And they are not religious issues—for war and hunger and ignorance and despair know no religious barriers.

But because I am a Catholic, and no Catholic has ever been elected president, the real issues in this campaign have been obscured—perhaps deliberately, in some quarters less responsible than this. So it is apparently necessary for me to state once again—not what kind of church I believe in, for that should be important only to me—but what kind of America I believe in.

I believe in an America where the separation of church and state is absolute—where no Catholic prelate would tell the president (should he be Catholic) how to act, and no Protestant minister would tell his parishoners for whom to vote—where no church or church school is granted any public funds or political preference—and where no man is denied public office merely because his religion differs from the president who might appoint him or the people who might elect him.

I believe in an America that is officially neither Catholic, Protestant nor Jewish—where no public official either requests or accepts instructions on public policy from the Pope, the National Council of Churches, or any other ecclesiastical source—where no religious body seeks to impose its will directly or indirectly upon the general populace or the public acts of its officials—and where religious liberty is so indivisible that an act against one church is treated as an act against all.

For while this year it may be a Catholic against whom the finger of suspicion is pointed, in other years it has been, and may someday be again, a Jew—or a Quaker—or a Unitarian—or a Baptist. It was Virginia's harassment of Baptist preachers, for example, that helped lead to Jefferson's statute of religious freedom. Today I may be the victim—but tomorrow it may be you—until the whole fabric of our harmonious society is ripped at a time of great national peril.

Finally, I believe in an America where religious intolerance will someday end—where all men and all churches are treated as equal—where every man has the same right to attend or not attend the church of his choice—where there is no Catholic vote, no anti-Catholic vote, no bloc voting of any kind—and where Catholics, Protestants, and Jews, at both the lay and pastoral level, will refrain from those attitudes of disdain and division which have so often marred their works in the past, and promote instead the American ideal of brotherhood.

That is the kind of America in which I believe. And it represents the kind of presidency in which I believe—a great office that must neither be humbled by making it the instrument of any one religious group nor tarnished by arbitrarily withholding its occupancy from the members of any one religious group. I believe in a president whose religious views are his own private affair, neither imposed by him upon the nation or imposed by the nation upon him as a condition to holding that office.

I would not look with favor upon a president working to subvert the first amendment's guarantees of religious liberty. Nor would our system of checks and balances permit him to do so—and neither do I look with favor upon those who would work to subvert Article VI of the Constitution by requiring a religious test—even by indirection—for it. If they disagree with that safeguard they should be out openly working to repeal it.

I want a chief executive whose public acts are responsible to all groups and obligated to none—who can attend any ceremony, service, or dinner his office may appropriately require of him—and whose fulfillment of his Presidential oath is not limited or conditioned by any religious oath, ritual or obligation.

This is the kind of America I believe in—and this is the kind I fought for in the South Pacific, and the kind my brother died for in Europe. No one suggested then that we may have a "divided loyalty," that we did "not believe in liberty," or that we belonged to a disloyal group that threatened the "freedoms for which our forefathers died."

And in fact this is the kind of America for which our forefathers died—when they fled here to escape religious test oaths that denied office to members of less favored churches—when they fought for the Constitution, the Bill of Rights, and the Virginia Statute of Religious Freedom—and when they fought at the shrine I visited today, the Alamo. For side by side with Bowie and Crockett died McCafferty and Bailey and Carey—but no one knows whether they were Catholic or not. For there was no religious test at the Alamo.

I ask you tonight to follow in that tradition—to judge me on the basis of my record of 14 years in Congress—on my declared stands against an ambassador to the Vatican, against unconstitutional aid to parochial schools, and against any boycott of the public schools (which I have attended myself)—instead of judging me on the basis of these pamphlets and publications we all have seen that carefully select quotations out of context from the statements of Catholic church leaders, usually in other countries, frequently in other centuries, and always omitting, of course, the statement of the American Bishops in 1948 which strongly endorsed church-state separation, and which more nearly reflects the views of almost every American Catholic.

DEMOCRATS! DEMOCRATS!

THE HARVARD LAW-GRADUATE DEMOCRATIC CLUB PRESENTS

A COLOSSAL

POLITICAL RALLY

SUPPORTING THE CANDIDACY OF

JOHN F. KENNEDY

NEXT PRESIDENT OF THESE UNITED STATES

☞ WITH 5 (Count Them) 5

MILITANTLY PARTISAN
SPEECHES

BY HIS MOST PROMINENT ADVISORS

★ JOHN K. GALBRAITH
★ MARK DeWOLFE HOWE
★ FRANCIS KEPPEL
★ W. W. ROSTOW
★ ARTHUR M. SCHLESINGER, JR.

Moderated By

ABRAM CHAYES

PATRIOTIC AIRS AND MARCHES
BY THE INCOMPARABLE
HARVARD UNIVERSITY BAND

SANDERS THEATRE

TUESDAY, NOVEMBER 1   8:00 P.M.

ADMISSION FREE!!

APPROVED — H. Y. D. C. — H. L. G. D. C.— NOVEMBER 2, 1960

This broadside advertises a Harvard "colossal political rally" with "5 militantly partisan speeches," including one by Arthur M. Schlesinger, jr.

I do not consider these other quotations binding upon my public acts—why should you? But let me say, with respect to other countries, that I am wholly opposed to the state being used by any religious group, Catholic or Protestant, to compel, prohibit, or persecute the free exercise of any other religion. And I hope that you and I condemn with equal fervor those nations which deny their presidency to Protestants and those which deny it to Catholics. And rather than cite the misdeeds of those who differ, I would cite the record of the Catholic Church in such nations as Ireland and France—and the independence of such statesmen as Adenauer and De Gaulle.

But let me stress again that these are my views—for contrary to common newspaper usage, I am not the Catholic candidate for president. I am the Democratic Party's candidate for president who happens also to be a Catholic. I do not speak for my church on public matters—and the church does not speak for me.

Whatever issue may come before me as president—on birth control, divorce, censorship, gambling, or any other subject—I will make my decision in accordance with these views, in accordance with what my conscience tells me to be the national interest, and without regard to outside religious pressures or dictates. And no power or threat of punishment could cause me to decide otherwise.

But if the time should ever come—and I do not concede any conflict to be even remotely possible—when my office would require me to either violate my conscience or violate the national interest, then I would resign the office; and I hope any conscientious public servant would do the same.

But I do not intend to apologize for these views to my critics of either Catholic or Protestant faith—nor do I intend to disavow either my views or my church in order to win this election.

If I should lose on the real issues, I shall return to my seat in the Senate, satisfied that I had tried my best and was fairly judged. But if this election is decided on the basis that 40 million Americans lost their chance of being president on the day they were baptized, then it is the whole nation that will be the loser, in the eyes of Catholics and non-Catholics around the world, in the eyes of history, and in the eyes of our own people.

But if, on the other hand, I should win the election, then I shall devote every effort of mind and spirit to fulfilling the oath of the Presidency— practically identical, I might add, to the oath I have taken for 14 years in the Congress. For without reservation, I can "solemnly swear that I will faithfully execute the office of President of the United States, and will to the best of my ability preserve, protect, and defend the Constitution . . . so help me God.

Kennedy's Inaugural Address

The 1960 election was one of the closest in history. Of the 68.8 million ballots cast, Kennedy won by 119,450—49.7 percent to Nixon's 49.6, with 0.7 percent going to minor parties. The Electoral College margin was more comfortable; Kennedy won 303 to 219, with 15 votes cast from Alabama, Mississippi, and Oklahoma for Senator Harry Byrd of Virginia.

John Kennedy personified a dramatic change in American politics. Handsome and athletic despite war injuries, he projected both grace and passion. Television now had enveloped America and Kennedy used the new medium like no other politician before him.

A blanket of seven inches of newly fallen snow, bitter winds, and subfreezing temperature held down the crowds that watched the inaugural ceremonies in front of the newly renovated East Front of the Capitol. As Richard Cardinal Cushing of Boston delivered the invocation asking Divine protection for the new president, a short circuit caused wisps of fine blue smoke to shoot out from under the lectern, almost as an ominous portent.

Vice President Johnson, Mr. Speaker, Mr. Chief Justice, President Eisenhower, Vice President Nixon, President Truman, reverend clergy, fellow citizens, we observe today not a victory of party, but a celebration of freedom—symbolizing an end, as well as a beginning—signifying renewal, as well as change. For I have sworn before you and Almighty God the same solemn oath our forebears prescribed nearly a century and three quarters ago.

The world is very different now. For man holds in his mortal hands the power to abolish all forms of human poverty and all forms of human life. And yet the same revolutionary beliefs for which our forebears fought are still at issue around the globe—the belief that the rights of man come not from the generosity of the state, but from the hand of God.

We dare not forget today that we are the heirs of that first revolution. Let the word go forth from this time and place, to friend and foe alike, that the torch has been passed to a new generation of Americans—born in this century, tempered by war, disciplined by a hard and bitter peace, proud of our ancient heritage—and unwilling to witness or permit the slow undoing of those human rights to which this Nation has always been committed, and to which we are committed today at home and around the world.

Let every nation know, whether it wishes us well or ill, that we shall pay any price, bear any burden, meet any hardship, support any friend, oppose any foe, in order to assure the survival and the success of liberty.

This much we pledge—and more.

To those old allies whose cultural and spiritual origins we share, we pledge the loyalty of faithful friends. United, there is little we cannot do in a host of cooperative ventures. Divided, there is little we can do—for we dare not meet a powerful challenge at odds and split asunder.

To those new States whom we welcome to the ranks of the free, we pledge our word that one form of colonial control shall not have passed away merely to be replaced by a far more iron tyranny. We shall not always expect to find them supporting our view. But we shall always hope to find them strongly supporting their own freedom—and to remember that, in the past, those who foolishly sought power by riding the back of the tiger ended up inside.

To those peoples in the huts and villages across the globe struggling to break the bonds of mass misery, we pledge our best efforts to help them help themselves, for whatever period is required—not because the Communists may be doing it, not because we seek their votes, but because it is right. If a free society cannot help the many who are poor, it cannot save the few who are rich.

To our sister republics south of our border, we offer a special pledge—to convert our good words into good deeds—in a new alliance for progress—to assist free men and free governments in casting off the chains of poverty. But this peaceful revolution of hope cannot become the prey of hostile powers. Let all our neighbors know that we shall join with them to oppose aggression or subversion anywhere in the Americas. And let every other power know that this Hemisphere intends to remain the master of its own house.

To that world assembly of sovereign states, the United Nations, our last best hope in an age where the instruments of war have far outpaced the instruments of peace, we renew our pledge of support—to prevent it from becoming merely a forum for invective—to strengthen its shield of the new and the weak—and to enlarge the area in which its writ may run.

Finally, to those nations who would make themselves our adversary, we offer not a pledge but a request: that both sides begin anew the quest for peace, before the dark powers of destruction unleashed by science engulf all humanity in planned or accidental self-destruction.

We dare not tempt them with weakness. For only when our arms are sufficient beyond doubt can we be certain beyond doubt that they will never be employed.

Poster for Kennedy and Johnson.

But neither can two great and powerful groups of nations take comfort from our present course—both sides overburdened by the cost of modern weapons, both rightly alarmed by the steady spread of the deadly atom, yet both racing to alter that uncertain balance of terror that stays the hand of mankind's final war.

So let us begin anew—remembering on both sides that civility is not a sign of weakness, and sincerity is always subject to proof. Let us never negotiate out of fear. But let us never fear to negotiate.

Let both sides explore what problems unite us instead of belaboring those problems which divide us.

Cardboard and silk lapel badge for Kennedy.

Let both sides, for the first time, formulate serious and precise proposals for the inspection and control of arms—and bring the absolute power to destroy other nations under the absolute control of all nations.

Let both sides seek to invoke the wonders of science instead of its terrors. Together let us explore the stars, conquer the deserts, eradicate disease, tap the ocean depths, and encourage the arts and commerce.

Let both sides unite to heed in all corners of the earth the command of Isaiah—to "undo the heavy burdens . . . and to let the oppressed go free."

And if a beachhead of cooperation may push back the jungle of suspicion, let both sides join in creating a new endeavor, not a new balance of power, but a new world of law, where the strong are just and the weak secure and the peace preserved.

All this will not be finished in the first 100 days. Nor will it be finished in the first 1,000 days, nor in the life of this Administration, nor even perhaps in our lifetime on this planet. But let us begin.

In your hands, my fellow citizens, more than in mine, will rest the final success or failure of our course. Since this country was founded, each generation of Americans has been summoned to give testimony to its national loyalty. The graves of young Americans who answered the call to service surround the globe.

Now the trumpet summons us again—not as a call to bear arms, though arms we need; not as a call to battle, though embattled we are—but a call to bear the burden of a long twilight struggle, year in and year out, "rejoicing in hope, patient in tribulation"—a struggle against the common enemies of man: tyranny, poverty, disease, and war itself.

Can we forge against these enemies a grand and global alliance, North and South, East and West, that can assure a more fruitful life for all mankind? Will you join in that historic effort?

In the long history of the world, only a few generations have been granted the role of defending freedom in its hour of maximum danger. I do not shrink from this responsibility—I welcome it. I do not believe that any of us would exchange places with any other people or any other generation. The energy, the faith, the devotion which we bring to this endeavor will light our country and all who serve it—and the glow from that fire can truly light the world.

And so, my fellow Americans: ask not what your country can do for you— ask what you can do for your country.

My fellow citizens of the world: ask not what America will do for you, but what together we can do for the freedom of man.

Finally, whether you are citizens of America or citizens of the world, ask of us the same high standards of strength and sacrifice which we ask of you. With a good conscience our only sure reward, with history the final judge of our deeds, let us go forth to lead the land we love, asking His blessing and His help, but knowing that here on earth God's work must truly be our own.

★ The Peace Corps ★

John Kennedy attracted an impressive number of
intellectuals and strategic thinkers to Washington. They
conceived of comprehensive plans for the Third World which
combined a vision of "modernization," (or "nation-building")
with counter-insurgency. The latter would use sophisticated
intelligence gathering methods—and the newly created
Special Forces or Green Berets—to thwart leftist operations.
"Nation-building" included the creation of economic
infrastructures, training of police and civil servants, and the
promotion of democratic institutions. Perhaps the most
striking part of this plan, the Peace Corps, came into existence
in the early days of the administration. On March 1, 1961,
Kennedy signed an Executive Order creating the Corps, to be
followed by Congressional action several months later. By
1963, 5,000 Americans had spread over the underdeveloped
world planning irrigation projects, purifying water, instructing
on the raising of better crops, and combating illiteracy.

I recommend to the Congress the establishment of a permanent Peace Corps—a pool of trained American men and women sent overseas by the U.S. Government or through private organizations and institutions to help foreign countries meet their urgent needs for skilled manpower.

I have today signed an Executive Order establishing a Peace Corps on a temporary pilot basis.

The temporary Peace Corps will be a source of information and experience to aid us in formulating more effective plans for a permanent organization. In addition, by starting the Peace Corps now we will be able to begin training young men and women for overseas duty this summer with the objective of placing them in overseas positions by late fall. This temporary Peace Corps is being established under existing authority in the Mutual Security Act and will be located in the Department of State. Its initial expenses will be paid from appropriations currently available for our foreign aid program.

Throughout the world the people of the newly developing nations are struggling for economic and social progress which reflects their deepest desires. Our own freedom, and the future of freedom around the world, depend, in a very real sense, on their ability to build growing and independent nations where men can live in dignity, liberated from the bonds of hunger, ignorance and poverty.

One of the greatest obstacles to the achievement of this goal is the lack of trained men and women with the skill to teach the young and assist in the operation of development projects—men and women with the capacity to cope with the demands of swiftly evolving economies, and with the dedication to put that capacity to work in the villages, the mountains, the towns and the factories of dozens of struggling nations.

The vast task of economic development urgently requires skilled people to do the work of the society—to help teach in the schools, construct development projects, demonstrate modern methods of sanitation in the villages, and perform a hundred other tasks calling for training and advanced knowledge.

To meet this urgent need for skilled manpower we are proposing the establishment of a Peace Corps—an organization which will recruit and train American volunteers, sending them abroad to work with the people of other nations.

This organization will differ from existing assistance programs in that its members will supplement technical advisers by offering the specific skills needed by developing nations if they are to put technical advice to work. They will help provide the skilled manpower necessary to carry out the development projects planned by the host governments, acting at a working level and serving at great personal sacrifice. There is little doubt that the number of those who wish to serve will be far greater than our capacity to absorb them. [. . .]

Most heartening of all, the initial reaction to this proposal has been an enthusiastic response by student groups, professional organizations and private citizens everywhere—a convincing demonstration that we have in this country an immense reservoir of dedicated men and women willing to devote their energies and time and toil to the cause of world peace and human progress.

Among the specific programs to which Peace Corps members can contribute are: teaching in primary and secondary schools, especially as part of national English language teaching programs; participation in the world-wide program of malaria eradication; instruction and operation of public health and sanitation projects; aiding in village development through school construction and other programs; increasing rural agricultural productivity by assisting local farmers to use modern implements and techniques. The initial emphasis of these programs will be on teaching. Thus the Peace Corps members will be an effective means of implementing the development programs of the host countries—programs which our technical assistance operations have helped to formulate.

The Peace Corps will not be limited to the young, or to college graduates. All Americans who are qualified will be welcome to join this effort. But undoubtedly the Corps will be made up primarily of young people as they complete their formal education. [. . .]

In all instances the men and women of the Peace Corps will go only to those countries where their services and skills are genuinely needed and desired. U.S. Operations Missions, supplemented where necessary by special Peace Corps teams, will consult with leaders in foreign countries in order to determine where Peace Corpsmen are needed, the types of jobs they can best fill, and the number of people who can be usefully employed. The Peace Corps will not supply personnel for marginal undertakings without a sound economic or social justification. In furnishing assistance through the Peace Corps careful regard will be given to the particular country's developmental priorities.

Membership in the Peace Corps will be open to all Americans, and applications will be available shortly. Where application is made directly to the Peace Corps—the vast majority of cases—they will be carefully screened to make sure that those who are selected can contribute to Peace Corps programs, and have the personal qualities which will enable them to represent the United States abroad with honor and dignity. In those cases where application is made directly to a private group, the same basic standards will be maintained. Each new recruit will receive a training and orientation period varying from six weeks to six months. This training will include courses in the culture and language of the country to which they are being sent and specialized training designed to increase the work skills of recruits. In some cases training will be conducted by participant agencies and universities in approved training programs. Other training programs will be conducted by the Peace Corps staff.

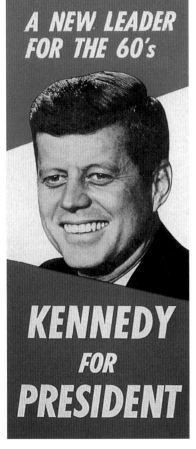

A NEW LEADER FOR THE 60's

KENNEDY FOR PRESIDENT

John Kennedy surrounded himself with youthful advisers. The members of the Kennedy team, David Halberstam would later write, "carried with them an exciting sense of American elitism, a sense that the best men had been summoned forth from the country." His administration, the president promised, would seek new solutions to old problems so as to get the country moving. However, the direction to which the country moved suggested how dependent Kennedy's approaches relied on the policies of his predecessors.

Length of service in the Corps will vary depending on the kind of project and the country, generally ranging from two to three years. Peace Corps members will often serve under conditions of physical hardship, living under primitive conditions among the people of developing nations. For every Peace Corps member service will mean a great financial sacrifice. They will receive no salary. Instead they will be given an allowance which will only be sufficient to meet their basic needs and maintain health. It is essential that Peace Corpsmen and women live simply and unostentatiously among the people they have come to assist. At the conclusion of their tours, members of the Peace Corps will receive a small sum in the form of severance pay based on length of service abroad, to assist them during their first weeks back in the United States. Service with the Peace Corps will not exempt volunteers from Selective Service.

The United States will assume medical responsibility for supplying medical services to Peace Corps members and ensuring supplies and drugs necessary to good health.

I have asked the temporary Peace Corps to begin plans and make arrangements for pilot programs. A minimum of several hundred volunteers could be selected, trained and at work abroad by the end of this calendar year. It is hoped that within a few years several thousand Peace Corps members will be working in foreign lands.

It is important to remember that the program must, in its early stages, be experimental in nature. This is a new dimension in our overseas program and only the most careful planning and negotiation can ensure its success.

The benefits of the Peace Corps will not be limited to the countries in which it serves. Our own young men and women will be enriched by the experience of living and working in foreign lands. They will have acquired new skills and experience which will aid them in their future careers and add to our own country's supply of trained personnel and teachers. They will return better able to assume the responsibilities of American citizenship and with greater understanding of our global responsibilities.

Although this is an American Peace Corps, the problem of world development is not just an American problem. Let us hope that other nations will mobilize the spirit and energies and skill of their people in some form of Peace Corps—making our own effort only one step in a major international effort to increase the welfare of all men and improve understanding among nations.

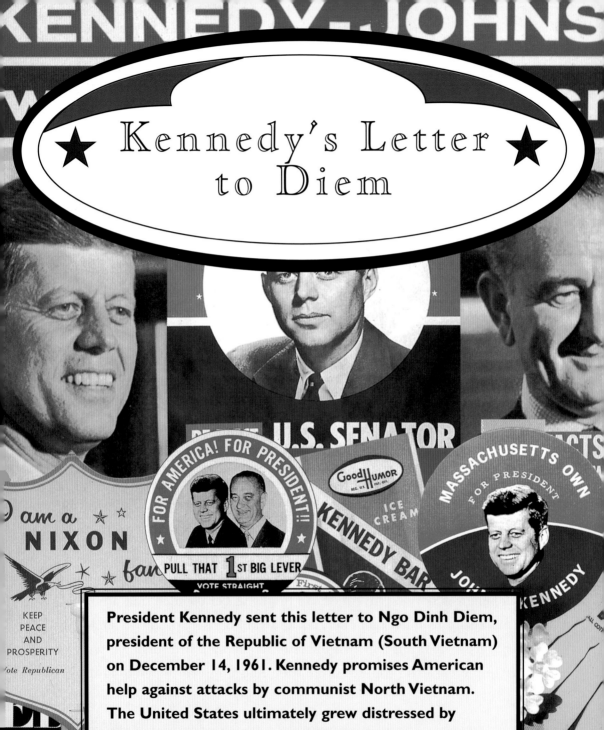

Kennedy's Letter to Diem

President Kennedy sent this letter to Ngo Dinh Diem, president of the Republic of Vietnam (South Vietnam) on December 14, 1961. Kennedy promises American help against attacks by communist North Vietnam. The United States ultimately grew distressed by Diem's corrupt regime; in 1963, the U.S. supported a coup that toppled Diem from power.

Dear Mr President:

I have received your recent letter in which you described so cogently the dangerous condition caused by North Vietnam's efforts to take over your country. The situation in your embattled country is well known to me and to the American people. We have been deeply disturbed by the assault on your country. Our indignation has mounted as the deliberate savagery of the Communist program of assassination, kidnapping, and wanton violence became clear.

Your letter underlines what our own information has convincingly shown—that the campaign of force and terror now being waged against your people and your government is supported and directed from the outside by the authorities at Hanoi. They have thus violated the provisions of the Geneva Accords designed to ensure peace in Vietnam and to which they bound themselves in 1954.

At that time, the United States, although not a party to the Accords, declared that it "would view any renewal of the aggression in violation of the Agreements with grave concern and as seriously threatening international peace and security." We continue to maintain that view.

In accordance with that declaration, and in response to your request, we are prepared to help the Republic of Vietnam to protect its people and to preserve its independence. We shall promptly increase our assistance to your defense effort as well as help relieve the destruction of the floods which you describe. I have already given the orders to get those programs underway.

The United States, like the Republic of Vietnam, remains devoted to the cause of peace and our primary purpose is to help your people maintain their independence. If the Communist authorities in North Vietnam will stop their campaign to destroy the Republic of Vietnam, the measures we are taking to assist your defense efforts will no longer be necessary. We shall seek to persuade the Communists to give up their attempts of force and subversion. In any case, we are confident that the Vietnamese people will preserve their independence and gain the peace and prosperity for which they have fought so hard and so long.

Two posters for Kennedy from the 1960 campaign.

In foreign affairs, President Kennedy warned that "we must never be lulled into believing that either [the Soviet Union or China] has yielded its ambitions for world domination." And, almost immediately, the new administration faced several crucial foreign policy situations. By spring 1961, American prestige had suffered two blows. In Laos, armed forces of the American-supported government gave ground before Soviet-backed rebels. In Cuba, Premier Fidel Castro, with military supplies and aid from the Russians, crushed a feeble American-supported effort of Cuban exiles to liberate their homeland. Meanwhile, hopes of any real agreement with the Soviet Union on disarmament languished. In the face of growing tension, Kennedy met with Premier Khrushchev in June 1961. The talks produced no agreements to ease the situation. Indeed, Khrushchev shortly demanded that the Western powers recognize East and West Germany as separate nations. The United States promptly increased its military strength in Berlin. Finally, in July 1963, after months of patient talks, the United States signed a nuclear test ban treaty with the Soviet Union—perhaps the greatest achievement of the Kennedy administration.

In Indochina, Kennedy shunned public debate (as had presidents Truman and Eisenhower) and relied only on a small group of advisers. Embracing Eisenhower's domino theory, Kennedy declared that a United States withdrawal "would mean a collapse not only of South Vietnam but Southeast Asia. So we are going to stay there." American military assistance soared to the floundering government of President Ngo Dinh Diem in South Vietnam. Kennedy doubled U.S. financial assistance, placed 16,500 additional military advisers there, and gave his approval to U.S. complicity in a coup that produced Diem's murder. The new government (the first of nine in the next five years) was given prompt American recognition.

Integrating the University of Mississippi

James Meredith was the first African American to be admitted to the University of Mississippi. After being rejected twice in 1961, he filed a federal complaint—that he had been denied admission because of his race. The Fifth Judicial Circuit Court ruled that the university maintained a policy of educational segregation. Nevertheless, Meredith's admission was opposed by state officials and most students. However, U.S. Attorney General Robert Kennedy sent federal marshals to the university to protect Meredith. Riots followed. Meredith continued to study at the university; he graduated in 1964. President Kennedy gave this televised report on the situation at the University of Mississippi on September 30, 1962.

The orders of the court in the case of *Meredith v. Fair* are beginning to be carried out. Mr. James Meredith is now in residence on the campus of the University of Mississippi.

This has been accomplished thus far without the use of National Guard or other troops. And it is to be hoped that the law enforcement officers of the State of Mississippi and the Federal marshals will continue to be sufficient in the future.

All students, members of the faculty, and public officials in both Mississippi and the Nation will be able, it is hoped, to return to their normal activities with full confidence in the integrity of American law.

This is as it should be, for our Nation is founded on the principle that observance of the law is the eternal safeguard of liberty and defiance of the law is the surest road to tyranny. The law which we obey includes the final rulings of the courts, as well as the enactments of our legislative bodies. Even among law-abiding men few laws are universally loved, but they are uniformly respected and not resisted.

Americans are free, in short, to disagree with the law but not to disobey it. For in a government of laws and not of men, no man, however prominent or powerful, and no mob however unruly or boisterous, is entitled to defy a court of law. If this country should ever reach the point where any man or group of men by force or threat of force could long defy the commands of our court and our Constitution, then no law would stand free from doubt, no judge would be sure of his writ, and no citizen would be safe from his neighbors.

In this case in which the United States Government was not until recently involved, Mr. Meredith brought a private suit in Federal court against those who were excluding him from the University. A series of Federal courts all the way to the Supreme Court repeatedly ordered Mr. Meredith's admission to the University. When those orders were defied, and those who sought to implement them were threatened with arrest and violence, the United States Court of Appeals consisting of Chief Judge Tuttle of Georgia, Judge Hutcheson of Texas, Judge Rives of Alabama, Judge Jones of Florida, Judge Brown of Texas, Judge Wisdom of Louisiana, Judge Gewin of Alabama, and Judge Bell of Georgia, made clear the fact that the enforcement of its order had become an obligation of the United States Government. Even though this Government had not originally been a party to the case, my responsibility as President was therefore inescapable. I accept it. My obligation under the Constitution and the statutes of the United States was and is to implement the orders of the court with whatever means are necessary, and with as little force and civil disorder as the circumstances permit.

It was for this reason that I federalized the Mississippi National Guard as the most appropriate instrument, should any be needed, to preserve law and order while United States marshals carried out the orders of the court and prepared to back them up with whatever other civil or military enforcement might have been required.

I deeply regret the fact that any action by the executive branch was necessary in this case, but all other avenues and alternatives, including persuasion and conciliation, had been tried and exhausted. Had the police powers of Mississippi been used to support the orders of the court, instead of deliberately and unlawfully blocking them, had the University of Mississippi fulfilled its standard of excellence by quietly admitting this applicant in conformity with what so many other southern State universities have done for so many years, a peaceable and sensible solution would have been possible without any Federal intervention.

This Nation is proud of the many instances in which governors, educators, and everyday citizens from the South have shown to the world the gains that can be made by persuasion and good will in a society ruled by law. Specifically, I would like to take this occasion to express the thanks of this Nation to those southerners who have contributed to the progress of our democratic development in the entrance of students regardless of race to such great institutions as the State-supported universities of Virginia, North Carolina, Georgia, Florida, Texas, Louisiana, Tennessee, Arkansas, and Kentucky.

I recognize that the present period of transition and adjustment in our Nation's Southland is a hard one for many people. Neither Mississippi nor any other southern State deserves to be charged with all the accumulated wrongs of the last 100 years of race relations. To the extent that there has been failure, the responsibility for that failure must be shared by us all, by every State, by every citizen.

Mississippi and her University, moreover, are noted for their courage, for their contribution of talent and thought to the affairs of this Nation. [. . .] In fact, the Guard unit federalized this morning, early, is part of the 155th Infantry, one of the 10 oldest regiments in the Union and one of the most decorated for sacrifice and bravery in 6 wars. [. . .]

I close therefore, with this appeal to the students of the University, the people who are most concerned.

You have a great tradition to uphold, a tradition of honor and courage won on the field of battle and on the gridiron as well as the University campus. You have a new opportunity to show that you are men of patriotism and integrity. For the most effective means of upholding the law is not the State policeman or the marshals or the National Guard. It is you. It lies in your courage to accept those laws with which you disagree as well as those with which you agree. The eyes of the Nation and of all the world are upon you and upon all of us, and the honor of your University and State are in the balance. I am certain that the great majority of the students will uphold that honor.

There is in short no reason why the books on this case cannot now be quickly and quietly closed in the manner directed by the court. Let us preserve both the law and the peace and then healing those wounds that are within we can turn to the greater crises that are without and stand united as one people in our pledge to man's freedom.

The Cuban Missile Crisis

The installation of Soviet nuclear missiles in Cuba confronted President Kennedy with the most wrenching test of his presidency. The crisis of October 1962, a thirteen-day ordeal, strengthened the president's determination to force the withdrawal of Soviet missiles from Cuba without war. Premier Nikita Khrushchev agreed to remove the missiles and to dismantle the launch sites. Kennedy gave written assurance that there would be no American invasion of Cuba. This was Kennedy's first, and most dangerous, foreign policy success.

The first document in this section is a transcript of Kennedy's October 22, 1962, address to the nation on the situation; the second is an October 28 letter from Kennedy to Khrushchev.

This Government, as promised, has maintained the closest surveillance of the Soviet military buildup on the island of Cuba. Within the past week, unmistakable evidence has established the fact that a series of offensive missile sites is now in preparation on that imprisoned island. The purpose of these bases can be none other than to provide a nuclear strike capability against the Western Hemisphere.

Upon receiving the first preliminary hard information of this nature last Tuesday morning at 9 A.M., I directed that our surveillance be stepped up. And having now confirmed and completed our evaluation of the evidence and our decision on a course of action, this Government feels obliged to report this new crisis to you in fullest detail.

The characteristics of these new missile sites indicate two distinct types of installations. Several of them include medium range ballistic missiles capable of carrying a nuclear warhead for a distance of more than 1,000 nautical miles. Each of these missiles, in short, is capable of striking Washington, D.C., the Panama Canal, Cape Canaveral, Mexico City, or any other city in the southeastern part of the United States, in Central America, or in the Caribbean area.

Additional sites not yet completed appear to be designed for intermediate range ballistic missiles—capable of traveling more than twice as far—and thus capable of striking most of the major cities in the Western Hemisphere, ranging as far north as Hudson Bay, Canada, and as far south as Lima, Peru. In addition, jet bombers, capable of carrying nuclear weapons, are now being uncrated and assembled in Cuba, while the necessary air bases are being prepared.

This urgent transformation of Cuba into an important strategic base—by the presence of these large, long range, and clearly offensive weapons of sudden mass destruction—constitutes an explicit threat to the peace and security of all the Americas, in flagrant and deliberate defiance of the Rio Pact of 1947, the traditions of this Nation and hemisphere, the joint resolution of the 87th Congress, the Charter of the United Nations, and my own public warnings to the Soviets on September 4 and 13. This action also contradicts the repeated assurances of Soviet spokesmen, both publicly and privately delivered, that the arms buildup in Cuba would retain its original defensive character, and that the Soviet Union had no need or desire to station strategic missiles on the territory of any other nation.

The size of this undertaking makes clear that it has been planned for some months. Yet only last month, after I had made clear the distinction between any introduction of ground-to-ground missiles and the existence of defensive antiaircraft missiles, the Soviet Government publicly stated on September 11, and I quote, "the armaments and military equipment sent to Cuba are designed exclusively for defensive purposes," that, and I quote the Soviet Government, "there is no need for the Soviet Government to shift its weapons . . . for a retaliatory blow to any other country, for instance Cuba," and that, and I quote their government, "the Soviet Union has so powerful rockets to carry these nuclear warheads that there is no need to search for sites for them beyond the boundaries of the Soviet Union." That statement was false.

Only last Thursday, as evidence of this rapid offensive buildup was already in my hand, Soviet Foreign Minister Gromyko told me in my office that he was instructed to make it clear once again, as he said his government had already done, that Soviet assistance to Cuba, and I quote, "pursued solely the purpose of contributing to the the defense capabilities of Cuba," that, and I quote him, "training by Soviet specialists of Cuban nationals in handling defensive armaments was by no means offensive, and if it were otherwise," Mr. Gromyko went on, "the Soviet Government would never become involved in rendering such assistance." That statement also was false.

Neither the United States of America nor the world community of nations can tolerate deliberate deception and offensive threats on the part of any nation, large or small. We no longer live in a world where only the actual firing of weapons represents a sufficient challenge to a nation's security to constitute maximum peril. Nuclear weapons are so destructive and ballistic missiles are so swift, that any substantially increased possibility of their use or any sudden change in their deployment may well be regarded as a definite threat to peace.

For many years both the Soviet Union and the United States, recognizing this fact, have deployed strategic nuclear weapons with great care, never upsetting the precarious status quo which insured that these weapons would not be used in the absence of some vital challenge. Our own strategic missiles have never been transferred to the territory of any other nation under a cloak of secrecy and deception; and our history—unlike that of the Soviets since the end of World War II—demonstrates that we have no desire to dominate or conquer any other nation or impose our system upon its people. Nevertheless, American citizens have become adjusted to living daily on the bull's-eye of Soviet missiles located inside the U.S.S.R. or in submarines.

In that sense, missiles in Cuba add to an already clear and present danger—although it should be noted the nations of Latin America have never previously been subjected to a potential nuclear threat.

But this secret, swift, and extraordinary buildup of Communist missiles— in an area well known to have a special and historical relationship to the United States and the nations of the Western Hemisphere, in violation of Soviet assurances, and in defiance of American and hemispheric policy—this sudden, clandestine decision to station strategic weapons for the first time outside of Soviet soil—is a deliberately provocative and unjustified change in the status quo which cannot be accepted by this country, if our courage and our commitments are ever to be trusted again by either friend or foe.

The 1930s taught us a clear lesson: aggressive conduct, if allowed to go unchecked and unchallenged ultimately leads to war. This nation is opposed to war. We are also true to our word. Our unswerving objective, therefore, must be to prevent the use of these missiles against this or any other country, and to secure their withdrawal or elimination from the Western Hemisphere.

Our policy has been one of patience and restraint, as befits a peaceful and powerful nation, which leads a worldwide alliance. We have been determined not to be diverted from our central concerns by mere irritants and fanatics. But now further action is required—and it is under way; and these actions may only be the beginning. We will not prematurely or unnecessarily risk the costs of worldwide nuclear war in which even the fruits of victory would be ashes in our mouth—but neither will we shrink from that risk at any time it must be faced.

Acting, therefore, in the defense of our own security and of the entire Western Hemisphere, and under the authority entrusted to me by the Constitution as endorsed by the resolution of the Congress, I have directed that the following initial steps be taken immediately:

First: To halt this offensive buildup, a strict quarantine on all offensive military equipment under shipment to Cuba is being initiated. All ships of any kind bound for Cuba from whatever nation or port will, if found to contain cargoes of offensive weapons, be turned back. This quarantine will be extended, if needed, to other types of cargo and carriers. We are not at this time, however, denying the necessities of life as the Soviets attempted to do in their Berlin blockade of 1948.

Second: I have directed the continued and increased close surveillance of Cuba and its military buildup. The foreign ministers of the OAS, in their communique of October 6, rejected secrecy in such matters in this hemisphere. Should these offensive military preparations continue, thus increasing the threat to the hemisphere, further action will be justified. I have directed the Armed Forces to prepare for any eventualities; and I trust that in the interest of both the Cuban people and the Soviet technicians at the sites, the hazards to all concerned in continuing this threat will be recognized.

Third: It shall be the policy of this Nation to regard any nuclear missile launched from Cuba against any nation in the Western Hemisphere as an attack by the Soviet Union on the United States, requiring a full retaliatory response upon the Soviet Union.

Fourth: As a necessary military precaution, I have reinforced our base at Guantanamo, evacuated today the dependents of our personnel there, and ordered additional military units to be on a standby alert basis.

Fifth: We are calling tonight for an immediate meeting of the Organ of Consultation under the Organization of American States, to consider this threat to hemispheric security and to invoke articles six and eight of the Rio Treaty in support of all necessary action. The United Nations Charter allows for regional security arrangements—and the nations of this hemisphere decided long ago against the military presence of outside powers. Our other allies around the world have also been alerted.

Sixth: Under the Charter of the United Nations, we are asking tonight that an emergency meeting of the Security Council be convoked without delay to take action against this latest Soviet threat to world peace. Our resolution will call for the prompt dismantling and withdrawal of all offensive weapons in Cuba, under the supervision of U.N. observers, before the quarantine can be lifted.

Seventh and finally: I call upon Chairman Khrushchev to halt and eliminate this clandestine, reckless, and provocative threat to world peace and to stable relations between our two nations. I call upon him further to abandon this course of world domination, and to join in an historic effort to end the perilous arms race and to transform the history of man. He has an opportunity now to move the world back from the abyss of destruction—by returning to his government's own words that it had no need to station missiles outside its own territory, and withdrawing these weapons from Cuba—by refraining from any action which will widen or deepen the present crisis—and then by participating in a search for peaceful and permanent solutions.

This Nation is prepared to present its case against the Soviet threat to peace, and our own proposals for a peaceful world, at any time and in any forum—in the OAS, in the United Nations, or in any other meeting that could be useful—without limiting our freedom of action. We have in the past made strenuous efforts to limit the spread of nuclear weapons. We have proposed the elimination of all arms and military bases in a fair and effective disarmament treaty. We are prepared to discuss new proposals for the removal of tensions on both sides—including the possibility of a genuinely independent Cuba, free to determine its own destiny. We have no wish to war with the Soviet Union—for we are a peaceful people who desire to live in peace with all other peoples.

But it is difficult to settle or even discuss these problems in an atmosphere of intimidation. That is why this latest Soviet threat—or any other threat which is made either independently or in response to our actions this week—must and will be met with determination. Any hostile move anywhere in the world against the safety and freedom of peoples to whom we are committed—including in particular the brave people of West Berlin—will be met by whatever action is needed.

Finally, I want to say a few words to the captive people of Cuba, to whom this speech is being directly carried by special radio facilities. I speak to you as a friend, as one who knows of your deep attachment to your fatherland, as one who shares your aspirations for liberty and justice for all. And I have watched and the American people have watched with deep sorrow how your nationalist revolution was betrayed— and how your fatherland fell under foreign domination. Now your leaders are no longer Cuban leaders inspired by Cuban ideals. They are puppets and agents of an international conspiracy which has turned Cuba against your friends and neighbors in the Americas— and turned it into the first Latin American country to become a target for nuclear war—the first Latin American country to have these weapons on its soil.

These new weapons are not in your interest. They contribute nothing to your peace and well-being. They can only undermine it. But this country has no wish to cause you to suffer or to impose any system upon you. We know that your lives and land are being used as pawns by those who deny your freedom.

Many times in the past, the Cuban people have risen to throw out tyrants who destroyed their liberty. And I have no doubt that most Cubans today look forward to the time when they will be truly free—free from foreign domination, free to choose their own leaders, free to select their own system, free to own their own land, free to speak and write and worship without fear or degradation. And then shall Cuba be welcomed back to the society of free nations and to the associations of this hemisphere.

My fellow citizens: let no one doubt that this is a difficult and dangerous effort on which we have set out. No one can see precisely what course it will take or what costs or casualties will be incurred. Many months of sacrifice and self-discipline lie ahead—months in which our patience and our will will be tested—months in which many threats and denunciations will keep us aware of our dangers. But the greatest danger of all would be to do nothing.

The path we have chosen for the present is full of hazards, as all paths are—but it is the one most consistent with our character and courage as a nation and our commitments around the world. The cost of freedom is always high—and Americans have always paid it. And one path we shall never choose, and that is the path of surrender or submission.

Our goal is not the victory of might, but the vindication of right—not peace at the expense of freedom, but both peace and freedom, here in this hemisphere, and, we hope, around the world. God willing, that goal will be achieved.

Thank you and good night.

Kennedy's Letter to Khrushchev, October 28, 1962

Dear Mr. Chairman:

I am replying at once to your broadcast message of 28 October even though the official text has not yet reached me because of the great importance I attach to moving forward promptly to the settlement of the Cuban crisis. I think that you and I, with our heavy responsibilities for the maintenance of peace, were aware that developments were approaching a point where events could have become unmanageable. So I welcome this message and consider it an important contribution to peace.

The distinguished efforts of Acting Secretary General U Thant have greatly facilitated both our tasks. I consider my letter to you of 27 October and your reply of today as firm undertakings on the part of both our governments which should be promptly carried out. I hope that the necessary measures can at once be taken through the United Nations as your message says, so that the United States in turn can remove the quarantine measures now in effect. I have already made arrangements to report all these matters to the Organization of American States, whose members share a deep interest in a genuine peace in the Caribbean area.

You referred in your letter to a violation of your frontier by an American aircraft in the area of the Chukotsk Peninsula. I have learned that this plane, without arms or photographic equipment, was engaged in an air sampling mission in connection with your nuclear tests. Its course was direct from Eielson Air Force Base in Alaska to the North Pole and return. In turning south, the pilot made a serious navigational error which carried him over Soviet territory. He immediately made an emergency call on open radio for navigational assistance and was guided back to his home base by the most direct route. I regret this incident and will see to it that every precaution is taken to prevent recurrence.

Mr. Chairman, both of our countries have great unfinished tasks and I know that your people as well as those of the United States can ask for nothing better than to pursue them free from the fear of war. Modern science and technology have given us the possibility of making labor fruitful beyond anything that could have been dreamed of a few decades ago.

I agree with you that we must devote urgent attention to the problem of disarmament, as it relates to the whole world and also to critical areas. Perhaps now, as we step back from danger, we can together make real progress in this vital field. I think we should give priority to questions relating to the proliferation of nuclear weapons, on earth and in outer space, and to the great effort for a nuclear test ban. But we should also work hard to see if wider measures of disarmament can be agreed and put into operation at an early date. The United States government will be prepared to discuss these questions urgently, and in a constructive spirit, at Geneva or elsewhere.

John F. Kennedy

Address to the Nation on Civil Rights

From the end of Reconstruction in 1877 to the early 1960s, three generations of the descendants of former slaves were denied equality as citizens as well as justice before the law. The first two years of the Kennedy administration were marked by violent racial clashes throughout the Old South. In the spring of 1963, Rev. Martin Luther King Jr. led massive demonstrations in Birmingham, Alabama. The nation watched on television as police used clubs and high-power fire hoses against them. Ku Klux Klan outrages increased. And, Alabama Governor George C. Wallace, promising "segregation today, segregation tomorrow, segregation forever," refused to allow the University of Alabama to admit its first black students. As a confrontation approached on June 11, 1963, President Kennedy ordered the Alabama State National Guard into federal service and that the students be enrolled. Although Governor Wallace backed down, he pledged unremitting defiance. That evening, Kennedy addressed the nation, speaking about race and civil rights more candidly than any of his predecessors.

This afternoon, following a series of threats and defiant statements, the presence of National Guardsmen was required on the University of Alabama to carry out the final and unequivocal order of the United States District Court of the Northern District of Alabama. That order called for the admission of two clearly qualified young Alabama residents who happened to have been born Negro.

That they were admitted peacefully on the campus is due in good measure to the conduct of the students of the University of Alabama, who met their responsibilities in a constructive way.

I hope that every American, regardless of where he lives, will stop and examine his conscience about this and other related incidents. This Nation was founded by men of many nations and backgrounds. It was founded on the principle that all men are created equal, and that the rights of every man are diminished when the rights of one man are threatened.

Today we are committed to a worldwide struggle to promote and protect the rights of all who wish to be free. And when Americans are sent to Vietnam or West Berlin, we do not ask for whites only. It ought to be possible, therefore, for American students of any color to attend any public institution they select without having to be backed up by troops.

It ought to be possible for American consumers of any color to receive equal service in places of public accommodation, such as hotels and restaurants and theaters and retail stores, without being forced to resort to demonstrations in the street, and it ought to be possible for American citizens of any color to register and to vote in a free election without interference or fear or reprisal.

It ought to be possible, in short, for every American to enjoy the privileges of being American without regard to his race or his color. In short, every American ought to have the right to be treated as he would wish to be treated, as one would wish his children to be treated. But this is not the case.

The Negro baby born in America today, regardless of the section of the Nation in which he is born, has about one-half as much chance as completing high school as a white baby born in the same place on the same day, one-third as much chance of becoming a professional man, twice as much chance of becoming unemployed, about one-seventh as much chance of earning $10,000 a year, a life expectancy which is seven years shorter, and the prospects of earning only half as much.

This is not a sectional issue. Difficulties over segregation and discrimination exist in every city, in every State of the Union, producing in many cities a rising tide of discontent that threatens the public safety. Nor is this a partisan issue. In a time of domestic crisis men of good will and generosity should be able to unite regardless of party or politics. This is not even a legal or legislative issue alone. It is better to settle these matters in courts than on the streets, and new laws are needed at every level, but law alone cannot make men see right.

We are confronted primarily with a moral issue. It is as old as the Scriptures and is as clear as the American Constitution.

The heart of the question is whether all Americans are to be afforded equal rights and equal opportunities, whether we are going to treat our fellow Americans as we want to be treated. If an American, because his skin is dark, cannot eat lunch in a restaurant open to the public, if he cannot send his children to the best public school available, if he cannot vote for the public officials who represent him, if, in short, he cannot enjoy the full and free life which all of us want, then who among us would be content to have the color of his skin changed and stand in his place? Who among us would then be content with the counsels of patience and delay?

One hundred years of delay have passed since President Lincoln freed the slaves, yet their heirs, their grandsons, are not fully free. [. . .] Now has come the time for this Nation to fulfill its promise. [. . .]

The fires of frustration and discord are burning in every city, North and

South, where legal remedies are not at hand. Redress is sought in the streets, in demonstrations, parades, and protests which create tensions and threaten violence and threaten lives.

We face, therefore, a moral crisis as a country and as a people. It cannot be met by repressive police action. It cannot be left to increased demonstrations in the streets. It cannot be quieted by token moves or talk. It is a time to act in the Congress, in your State and local legislative body and, above all, in all of our daily lives.

It is not enough to pin the blame on others, to say this is a problem of one section of the country or another, or deplore the fact that we face. A great change is at hand, and our task, our obligation, is to make that revolution, that change, peaceful and constructive for all.

Those who do nothing are inviting shame as well as violence. Those who act boldly are recognizing right as well as reality.

Next week I shall ask the Congress of the United States to act, to make a commitment it has not fully made in this century to the proposition that race has no place in American life or law. The Federal judiciary has upheld that proposition in a series of forthright cases. The executive branch has adopted that proposition in the conduct of its affairs, including the employment of Federal personnel, the use of Federal facilities, and the sale of federally financed housing.

But there are other necessary measures which only the Congress can provide, and they must be provided at this session. The old code of equity law under which we live commands for every wrong a remedy, but in too many communities, in too many parts of the country, wrongs are inflicted on Negro citizens and there are no remedies at law. Unless Congress acts, their only remedy is in the street.

I am, therefore, asking the Congress to enact legislation giving all Americans the right to be served in facilities which are open to the public— hotels, restaurants, theaters, retail stores, and similar establishments.

This seems to me to be an elementary right. Its denial is an arbitrary indignity that no American in 1963 should have to endure, but many do.

I have recently met with scores of business leaders urging them to take voluntary action to end this discrimination and I have been encouraged by their response, and in the last two weeks over 75 cities have seen progress made in desegregating these kinds of facilities. But many are unwilling to act alone, and for this reason, nationwide legislation is needed if we are to move this problem from the streets to the courts.

I am also asking Congress to authorize the Federal Government to participate more fully in lawsuits designed to end segregation in public education. We have succeeded in persuading many districts to desegregate voluntarily. Dozens have admitted Negroes without violence. Today a Negro is attending a State-supported institution in every one of our 50 states, but the pace is very slow.

Too many Negro children entering segregated grade schools at the time of the Supreme Court's decision nine years ago will enter segregated high schools this fall, having suffered a loss which can never be restored. The lack of an adequate education denies the Negro a chance to get a decent job.

The orderly implementation of the Supreme Court decision, therefore, cannot be left solely to those who may not have the economic resources to carry the legal action or who may be subject to harassment.

Other features will also be requested, including greater protection for the right to vote. But legislation, I repeat, cannot solve this problem alone. It must be solved in the homes of every American in every community across our country.

In this respect, I want to pay tribute to those citizens North and South who have been working in their communities to make a better life for all. They are acting not out of a sense of legal duty but out of a sense of human decency.

Like our soldiers and sailors in all parts of the world they are meeting freedom's challenge on the firing line, and I salute them for their honor and their courage.

My fellow Americans, this is a problem which faces us all—in every city of the North as well as the South. Today there are Negroes unemployed, two or three times as many compared to whites, inadequate in education, moving into the large cities, unable to find work, young people particularly out of work without hope, denied equal rights, denied the opportunity to eat at a restaurant or lunch counter or go to a movie theater, denied the right to a decent education, denied almost today the right to attend a State university even though qualified. It seems to me that these are matters which concern us all, not merely presidents or congressmen or governors, but every citizen of the United States.

This is one country. It has become one country because all of us and all the people who came here had an equal chance to develop their talents.

We cannot say to 10 percent of the population that you can't have that right; that your children can't have the chance to develop whatever talents they have; that the only way that they are going to get their rights is to go into the street and demonstrate. I think we owe them and we owe ourselves a better country than that.

Therefore, I am asking for your help in making it easier for us to move ahead and to provide the kind of equality of treatment which we would want ourselves; to give a chance for every child to be educated to the limit of his talents.

As I have said before, not every child has an equal talent or an equal ability or an equal motivation, but they should have the equal right to develop their talent and their ability and their motivation, to make something of themselves.

We have a right to expect that the Negro community will be responsible, will uphold the law, but they have a right to expect that the law will be fair, that the Constitution will be color blind, as Justice Harlan said at the turn of the century.

This is what we are talking about and this is a matter which concerns this country and what it stands for, and in meeting it I ask the support of all our citizens.

"Ich bin ein Berliner"

In June 1963, President Kennedy began a goodwill tour to western Europe. The first stop was Berlin, which since the Second World War had become the focus of tension between the United States and the Soviet Union. In 1961, a 12-foot-high wall had been built through the city. The wall was the symbolic division between communist (and Soviet-controlled) East Germany and the democratic republic of West Germany. On June 26, a large and enthusiastic crowd gathered near the Berlin Wall to hear Kennedy deliver this memorable speech.

I am proud to come to this city as the guest of your distinguished Mayor, who has symbolized throughout the world the fighting spirit of West Berlin. And I am proud to visit the Federal Republic with your distinguished Chancellor who for so many years has committed Germany to democracy and freedom and progress, and to come here in the company of my fellow American, General Clay, who has been in this city during its great moments of crisis and will come again if ever needed.

Two thousand years ago the proudest boast was "civis Romanus sum." Today, in the world of freedom, the proudest boast is "Ich bin ein Berliner."

I appreciate my interpreter translating my German!

There are many people in the world who really don't understand, or say they don't, what is the great issue between the free world and the Communist world. Let them come to Berlin. There are some who say that communism is the wave of the future. Let them come to Berlin. And there are some who say in Europe and elsewhere we can work with the Communists. Let them come to Berlin. And there are even a few who say that it is true that communism is an evil system, but it permits us to make economic progress. *Lass' sie nach Berlin kommen.* Let them come to Berlin.

Freedom has many difficulties and democracy is not perfect, but we have never had to put a wall up to keep our people in, to prevent them from leaving us. I want to say, on behalf of my countrymen, who live many miles away on the other side of the Atlantic, who are far distant from you, that they take the greatest pride that they have been able to share with you, even from a distance, the story of the last 18 years. I know of no town, no city, that has been besieged for 18 years that still lives with the vitality and the force, and the hope and the determination of the city of West Berlin. While the wall is the most obvious and vivid demonstration of the failures of the Communist system, for all the world to see, we take no

Kennedy's pledge to "get America moving again" inspired a variety of campaign items which used the theme of leadership. Others utilized Kennedy's "New Frontier" slogan.

In the last Gallup Poll dealing with Kennedy's approval rating, conducted between October 11–16, 1963, 59 percent approved of the way "John Kennedy is handling his job as President"—57 percent of men and 61 percent of women. Those between 21–29 years, approved of the president 68 percent compared to 53 percent in the "50-years and over" group. Eighty-five percent of "non-whites" approved of Kennedy's job performance with 55 percent in the "whites only" category. Catholics approved of the president by 78 percent while this rating drops to 52 percent among Protestants.

FACTS FOR NEW YORK VOTERS:

KENNEDY
FOR PRESIDENT

A TIME FOR GREATNESS

U. S. SENATOR
JOHN F.
KENNEDY
FOR
PRESIDENT

YOUTH FOR KENNEDY

satisfaction in it, for it is, as your Mayor has said, an offense not only against history but an offense against humanity, separating families, dividing husbands and wives and brothers and sisters, and dividing a people who wish to be joined together.

What is true of this city is true of Germany—real, lasting peace in Europe can never be assured as long as one German out of four is denied the elementary right of free men, and that is to make a free choice. In 18 years of peace and good faith, this generation of Germans has earned the right to be free, including the right to unite their families and their nation in lasting peace, with good will to all people. You live in a defended island of freedom, but your life is part of the main. So let me ask you as I close, to lift your eyes beyond the dangers of today, to the hopes of tomorrow, beyond the freedom merely of this city of Berlin, or your country of Germany, to the advance of freedom everywhere, beyond the wall to the day of peace with justice, beyond yourselves and ourselves to all mankind.

Freedom is indivisible, and when one man is enslaved, all are not free. When all are free, then we can look forward to that day when this city will be joined as one and this country and this great Continent of Europe in a peaceful and hopeful globe. When that day finally comes, as it will, the people of West Berlin can take sober satisfaction in the fact that they were in the front lines for almost two decades.

All free men, wherever they may live, are citizens of Berlin, and, therefore, as a free man, I take pride in the words "Ich bin ein Berliner."

★ The Assassination of Kennedy ★

On November 22, 1963, while riding in a motorcade through the streets of Dallas, President Kennedy was shot and killed. The assassination traumatized the nation. Lee Harvey Oswald was arrested for the murder, but Oswald himself was killed before he could be indicted for the crime.

The following is the statement President Lyndon B. Johnson gave to the Warren Commission, which investigated the assassination. Johnson recalled the events of the day. The commission's report, which concluded that Oswald had acted alone, has never been fully accepted by the public.

Friday morning, November 22, began with a reception in the Longhorn Room of the Hotel Texas, Fort Worth. President and Mrs. Kennedy and Mrs. Johnson and I had spent the night in that hotel. Then, President Kennedy and I went to a parking lot across from the hotel where a speaker's stand had been set up and we addressed a crowd that was gathered there. We then returned to the hotel and had breakfast.

After that, at about 10:30 A.M. we motored to the Fort Worth airfield. Mrs. Johnson and I then went aboard *Air Force II* for the trip to Dallas. We arrived at Love Field in Dallas, as I remember, just shortly after 11:30 A.M. Agents Youngblood and Johns and two other agents were with us.

We disembarked from the plane promptly after it came to a stop at Love Field. We were met by a committee of local officials and citizens. After greeting them, Mrs. Johnson and I, together with the special agents, walked over to the area where President and Mrs. Kennedy would disembark. We were followed by the reception committee.

President Kennedy's plane arrived about 5 or 10 minutes after *Air Force II*. The President and Mrs. Kennedy disembarked and they greeted us and the people in the reception committee.

Then the President and Mrs. Kennedy walked along the fence, shaking hands with people in the crowd that had assembled. Mrs. Johnson and I followed along the fence, greeting people and shaking hands. This took 5 or 10 minutes, as I recall.

Mrs. Johnson, Senator Ralph Yarborough, and I then entered the car which had been provided for us in the motorcade. It was a Lincoln Continental convertible. I think that our car was the fourth in the motorcade. We were the second car behind the President's automobile.

The driver of the car in which Mrs. Johnson and I were riding was Hurchel Jacks, who is a member of the Texas State Highway Patrol. Agent Youngblood was sitting next to him in the front seat.

I was sitting behind Agent Youngblood; Mrs. Johnson was next to me; and Senator Yarborough was on the left of the rear seat—that is, just behind the driver.

At first, as we left Love Field and proceeded through the less-populated areas, the crowds were thin. I recall, however, that Mrs. Johnson and I and Senator Yarborough commented upon the good spirit and obvious good wishes of the crowd. As we drove closer to town, the crowds became quite large.

We made several stops as a result of stops by the automobiles ahead of us. I did not get out of the car, but on occasion a few people broke from the crowd and ran over, and I shook hands with several people on these occasions.

The motorcade proceeded down Main Street and then turned right on Houston. It then turned into Elm, which is a block, I believe, beyond the intersection of Main and Houston. The crowd on Elm Street was smaller.

As the motorcade proceeded down Elm Street to the point where the assassination occurred, it was traveling at a speed which I should estimate at 12 or 15 miles and hour.

After we had proceeded a short way down Elm Street, I heard a sharp report. The crowd at this point had become somewhat spotty.

The Vice-Presidential car was then about three car lengths behind President Kennedy's car, with the Presidential followup car intervening.

I was startled by the sharp report or explosion. but I had no time to speculate as to its origin because Agent Youngblood turned in a flash, immediately after the first explosion, hitting me on the shoulder, and shouted to all of us in the back seat to get down. I was pushed down by Agent Youngblood. Almost in the same moment in which he hit or pushed me, he vaulted over the back seat and sat on me. I was bent over under the weight of Agent Youngblood's body, toward Mrs. Johnson and Senator Yarborough.

I remember attempting to turn my head to make sure that Mrs. Johnson had bent down. Both she and Senator Yarborough had crouched down at Agent Youngblood's command.

At some time in this sequence of events. I heard other explosions. It was impossible for me to tell the direction from which the explosions came.

I felt the automobile sharply accelerate, and in a moment or so Agent Youngblood released me. I ascertained that Mrs. Johnson and Senator Yarborough were all right. I heard Agent Youngblood speaking over his radio transmitter. I asked him what had happened. He said that he was not sure but that he had learned that the motorcade was going to the hospital.

I did not see anything that was going on in and around the President's automobile.

When we arrived at the hospital; Agent Youngblood told me to get out of the car, go into the building, not to stop, and to stay close to him and the other agents. When the car came to a stop. a cordon of agents formed around me, and we walked rapidly into the hospital and then we went into a room there.

Because of the method which Agent Youngblood directed for leaving the car and entering the hospital, I did not see the Presidential car or any of the persons in it.

In the hospital room to which Mrs. Johnson and I were taken, the shades were drawn—I think by Agent Youngblood. In addition to him, two or three other agents were there.

As I remember, we got our first specific report from Emory Roberts, one of the agents from the White House detail. He told us that President Kennedy had been very badly injured and that his condition was quite poor. He said that he thought we should make plans to get back to Washington immediately.

I asked about Governor Connally and was told that he, too, had been shot, but that his wound was not serious. I was told that Mrs. Kennedy and Mrs. Connally were uninjured and that no one else had been hurt.

Mrs. Johnson and I asked if we could see Mrs. Kennedy and Mrs. Connally. Agent Youngblood told me that I could not leave the room, and I followed his direction.

In honor of
President John F. Kennedy
and
Vice President Lyndon B. Johnson

The State Democratic Executive Committee
requests the pleasure of your company
at the
Texas Welcome Dinner
on Friday evening the twenty-second of November
One thousand nine hundred and sixty-three
at half after seven o'clock
at the Municipal Auditorium
in the City of Austin

Contribution card enclosed
Optional dress

Mr. Eugene M. Locke, Chairman
Mrs. Alfred Negley, Vice-Chairman
Mr. Frank C. Erwin, Jr., Secretary

Invitation to the Texas Welcome Dinner, November 22, 1963, in Austin. Kennedy was killed in Dallas a few hours earlier.

Mrs. Johnson was allowed to leave for this purpose.

At some time during these events, Kenneth O'Donnell, Congressman Jack Brooks, Congressman Homer Thornberry, and Cliff Carter came into the room.

It was Ken O'Donnell who, at about 1:20 P.M., told us that the President had died. I think his precise words were, "He's gone." O'Donnell said that we should return to Washington and that we should take the President's plane for this purpose.

I found it hard to believe that this had happened. The whole thing seemed unreal—unbelievable. A few hours earlier, I had breakfast with John Kennedy; he was alive, strong, vigorous. I could not believe now that he was dead. I was shocked and sickened.

When Mr. O'Donnell told us to get on the plane and go back to Washington, I asked about Mrs. Kennedy. O'Donnell told me that Mrs. Kennedy would not leave the hospital without the President's body, and urged again that we go ahead and and take *Air Force I* and return to Washington.

I did not want to go and leave Mrs. Kennedy in this situation. I said so, but I agreed that we would board the airplane and wait until Mrs. Kennedy and the President's body were brought aboard the plane.

It is, of course, difficult to convey an accurate impression of the period of time that we were in the hospital room. We were all stunned. I suppose we were in a state of shock and there was no time for the shock to wear off sufficiently so that the magnitude of our personal loss of this great man and good friend could express itself in words or in surface feelings.

I suppose, actually, that the only outlet for the grief that shock had submerged was our sharp, painful, and bitter concern and solicitude for Mrs. Kennedy.

Despite my awareness of the reasons for Mr. O'Donnell's insistence—in which I think he was joined by one or more of the Secret Service agents—that we board the airplane, leave Dallas, and go to Washington without delay, I was determined that we would not return until Mrs. Kennedy was ready, and that we would carry the President's body back with us if she wanted.

We left the room and were ushered by a cordon of agents to cars which were awaiting us. At Agent Youngblood's insistence, I entered one car and Mrs. Johnson another. Agent Youngblood and I were sitting in the back seat and Congressman Thornberry was in the front seat.

As we started away from the hospital, Congressman Albert Thomas came up to the car. He saw Congressman Thornberry—I don't think he saw me—and he asked the Congressman to wait for him. At my direction, the car stopped and picked him up and he sat in the front seat with Congressman Thornberry. I am sure this didn't take as much as minute. Congressman Thornberry then climbed over and got into the back seat with us.

When we got to the airport, we proceeded to drive to the ramp leading into the plane, and we entered the plane.

We were ushered into the private quarters of the President's plane. It didn't seem right for John Kennedy not to be there. I told someone that we preferred for Mrs. Kennedy to use these quarters.

Shortly after we boarded the plane. I called Robert Kennedy, the President's brother and the Attorney General. I knew how grief-stricken he was, and I wanted to say something that would comfort him. Despite his shock, he discussed the practical problems at hand—problems of special urgency because we did not at that time have any information as to the motivation of the assassination or its possible implications. The Attorney General said that he would like to look into the matter of whether the oath of office as President should be administered to me immediately or after we returned to Washington, and that he would call back.

I thereafter talked with McGeorge Bundy and Walter Jenkins, both of whom urged that the return to Washington should not be delayed. I told them I was waiting for Mrs. Kennedy and for the President's body to be placed on the plane, and would not return prior to that time.

As I remember, our conversation was interrupted to allow the Attorney General to come back on the line. He said that the oath should be administered to me immediately, before taking off for Washington, and that it should be administered by a judicial officer of the United States. Shortly thereafter, the Deputy Attorney General, Mr. Katzenbach, dictated the form of oath to one of the secretaries aboard the plane.

I thought of Sarah Hughes, an old friend who is judge of the U.S. district court in Dallas. We telephoned Judge Hughes' office. She was not there, but she returned the call in a few minutes and said she would be at the airplane in 10 minutes. I asked that arrangements be made to permit her to have access to the airplane.

A few minutes later Mrs. Kennedy and the President's coffin arrived. Mrs. Johnson and I spoke to her. We tried to comfort her, but our words seemed inadequate. She went into the private quarters of the plane. I estimate that Mrs. Kennedy and the coffin arrived about a half hour after we entered the plane just after 2 o'clock.

About a half hour later, I asked someone to find out if Mrs. Kennedy would stand with us during the administration of the oath. Mrs. Johnson went back to be with her. Mrs. Kennedy came and stood with us during the moments that the oath was being administered.

I shall never forget her bravery, nobility, and dignity.

I'm told that the oath was administered at 2:40 P.M. Mrs. Johnson and Mrs. Kennedy were at my side as Judge Hughes administered the oath of office.

The plane took off promptly after the swearing-in ceremonies. I then called

Figurines of the President's children, Caroline and John Kennedy Jr., circa 1964.

Overall, assassinations and direct attempts on the life of the president since the founding of the nation through 2002 affected eight presidents while they were in office. Four presidents (Abraham Lincoln, James Garfield, William McKinley, and John Kennedy) have been shot to death, while another four have been exposed either to assailants' bullets (Andrew Jackson, Gerald Ford, and Ronald Reagan) or to an armed attack on their official residence (Harry Truman). Only one president (Ford) has been the target of more than one assassination attempt.

President Kennedy's mother, Mrs. Rose Kennedy. She had previously been advised of the assassination. I told her of our grief and of our sorrow for her. I gave the telephone to Mrs. Johnson, who also tried to bring a word of comfort to the President's mother. I then called Nellie Connally, the Governor's wife, and told her of our concern for her and John, and tried to give her some comfort.

I then asked General Clifton, the military aide to the President, to call McGeorge Bundy in Washington to instruct him to ask the Cabinet members who were on their way to Japan to return immediately.

When we landed at the Andrews Air Force Base, I made a short statement for the press, radio, and television. In my heart, I asked for God's help that I should not prove unworthy of the responsibility which fate had thrust upon me.

Further Reading

GENERAL REFERENCE

Israel, Fred L. *Student's Atlas of American Presidential Elections, 1789–1996*. Washington, D.C.: Congressional Quarterly Books, 1998.

Levy, Peter B., editor. *100 Key Documents in American History*. Westport, Conn.: Praeger, 1999.

Mieczkowski, Yarek. *The Routledge Historical Atlas of Presidential Elections*. New York: Routledge, 2001.

Polsby, Nelson W., and Aaron Wildavsky. *Presidential Elections: Strategies and Structures of American Politics*. 10th edition. New York: Chatham House, 2000.

Watts, J. F., and Fred L. Israel, editors. *Presidential Documents*. New York: Routledge, 2000.

Widmer, Ted. *The New York Times Campaigns: A Century of Presidential Races*. New York: DK Publishing, 2000.

POLITICAL AMERICANA REFERENCE

Cunningham, Noble E. Jr. *Popular Images of the Presidency: From Washington to Lincoln*. Columbia: University of Missouri Press, 1991.

Melder, Keith. *Hail to the Candidate: Presidential Campaigns from Banners to Broadcasts*. Washington, D.C.: Smithsonian Institution Press, 1992.

Schlesinger, Arthur M. jr., Fred L. Israel, and David J. Frent. *Running for President: The Candidates and their Images*. 2 vols. New York: Simon and Schuster, 1994.

Warda, Mark. *100 Years of Political Campaign Collectibles*. Clearwater, Fla.: Galt Press, 1996.

THE ELECTION OF 1960
and the Administration of John F. Kennedy

Dover, E. D. *Presidential Elections in the Television Age, 1960–1992*. Westport, Conn.: Praeger Publishing, 1994.

Fursenko, Aleksandr, and Timothy Naftali. *"One Hell of a Gamble": Khrushchev, Castro, and Kennedy, 1958–1964*. New York: W.W. Norton, 1997.

Gellman, Irwin F. *The Contender: Richard Nixon, the Congress Years, 1946–1952*. New York: Free Press, 1999.

Kallina, Edmund. *Courthouse over White House: Chicago and the Presidential Election of 1960*. Gainesville: University Press of Florida, 1988.

Leamer, Laurence. *The Kennedy Men, 1901–1963*. New York: William Morrow, 2001.

Livingstone, Harrison Edward, and Robert J. Groden. *High Treason: The Assassination of JFK and the Case for Conspiracy*. New York: Carroll and Graf, 1998.

McGillivray, Alice V., Richard M. Scammon, and Rhodes Cook. *America at the Polls 1960–1996: Kennedy to Clinton: A Handbook of American Presidential Election Statistics*. Washington, D.C.: Congressional Quarterly, 1998.

Mahoney, Richard D. *The Days of Jack and Bobby Kennedy*. New York: Arcade Publishing, 2000.

Nixon, Richard M. *RN: The Memoirs of Richard Nixon*. Carmichael, Calif.: Touchstone Books, 1990.

Perret, Geoffrey. *Jack: A Life Like No Other*. New York: Random House, 2001.

Reeves, Thomas C. *A Question of Character: A Life of John F. Kennedy*. New York: The Free Press, 1991.

Weisbrot, Robert. *Maximum Danger: Kennedy, the Missiles, and the Crisis of American Confidence*. Chicago: Ivan R. Dee, 2001.

White, Theodore H. *The Making of the President 1960*. New York: Atheneum Publishers, 1961.

INDEX

Numbers in **bold italics** refer to captions.

The EDITORS

ARTHUR M. SCHLESINGER JR. holds the Albert Schweitzer Chair in the Humanities at the Graduate Center of the City University of New York. He is the author of more than a dozen books, including *The Age of Jackson; The Vital Center; The Age of Roosevelt* (3 vols.); *A Thousand Days: John F. Kennedy in the White House; Robert Kennedy and His Times; The Cycles of American History;* and *The Imperial Presidency.* Professor Schlesinger served as Special Assistant to President Kennedy (1961–63). His numerous awards include: the Pulitzer Prize for History; the Pulitzer Prize for Biography; two National Book Awards; The Bancroft Prize; and the American Academy of Arts and Letters Gold Medal for History.

FRED L. ISRAEL is professor emeritus of American history, City College of New York. He is the author of *Nevada's Key Pittman* and has edited *The War Diary of Breckinridge Long* and *Major Peace Treaties of Modern History, 1648–1975* (5 vols.) He holds the Scribe's Award from the American Bar Association for his joint editorship of the *Justices of the United States Supreme Court* (4 vols.). For more than 25 years Professor Israel has compiled and edited the Gallup Poll into annual reference volumes.

DAVID J. FRENT is the president of Political Americana Auctions, Oakhurst, NJ. With his wife, Janice, he has assembled the nation's foremost private collection of political campaign memorabilia. Mr. Frent has designed exhibits for corporations, the Smithsonian Institution, and the United States Information Agency. A member of the board of directors of the American Political Items Collectors since 1972, he was elected to its Hall of Fame for his "outstanding contribution to preserving and studying our political heritage."